Master of Games

by

Michael A Neil Jr.

Front Matter

To the architects of dread, the weavers of shadow, and the minds that dare to explore the labyrinthine corridors of human darkness. This story is an homage to the late-night epiphanies that bloom in the quiet hours, to the thrill of unraveling a meticulously crafted enigma, and to the chilling realization that the most dangerous monsters often wear the most unassuming masks. It is for those who find beauty in the complex tapestry of motive, for those who appreciate the subtle, creeping tendrils of unease that snake through the ordinary, and for those who understand that sometimes, the most profound truths are found not in the light, but in the suffocating embrace of the unseen. May your own nights be filled with intellectual pursuits, and may your skepticism be as sharp as your intuition. This one is for you, fellow travelers in the shadowed realms of the human psyche, for you who understand that the greatest mysteries are not always those of whodunit, but of *why* and *how* the human heart can be so exquisitely, terrifyingly broken. To the readers who crave a story that lingers, that whispers in the quiet moments, and that forces you to question the very fabric of perception and control. May you find yourselves lost within these pages, only to emerge, perhaps a little more aware, a little more wary, but undeniably, utterly, consumed by the chase.

Chapter 1: The Lure of the Unseen

The hushed sanctity of the Grand Athenaeum library was Adam Tapper's universe. Not the grand, sunlit reading rooms where scholars debated and students hunched over textbooks, but the forgotten, dust-choked archives in the sub-basement. Here, where the air hung heavy with the scent of decaying paper and the silent screams of forgotten narratives, Adam felt most at home. His life was a meticulously cataloged existence, each day a predictable sequence of shelving, indexing, and the quiet hum of fluorescent lights reflecting off worn leather spines. He moved through the aisles with a silent, almost spectral grace, a ghost in a kingdom of stories.

Adam was a man defined by his solitude, a deliberate cloistering that had begun in childhood. He'd always been the observer, the boy on the periphery, absorbing the world through a lens of detached analysis. This distance, however, was a double-edged sword. While it granted him an almost preternatural ability to perceive the subtle currents of human interaction, it also bred a profound sense of inadequacy. He was a spectator in the grand theater of life, forever relegated to the wings, yearning for a spotlight he felt he was too awkward, too plain, too *unremarkable* to ever command. This gnawing inferiority was a constant companion, a dark shadow that clung to him even in the brightest of rooms. To combat it, he cultivated an intellectual superiority complex, a shield forged from obscure knowledge and a condescending smirk reserved for those who dared to engage with him on intellectual matters. He devoured books not for pleasure, but for power, meticulously collecting facts and theories like a dragon hoarding gold, believing that knowledge was the ultimate weapon against his own perceived deficiencies.

His preferred domain, the sub-basement archives, was a labyrinth of towering shelves crammed with forgotten tomes, their titles faded, their bindings cracked. It was a place where time itself seemed to have slowed, where the whispers of centuries settled like fine dust. He knew every alcove, every cobweb-draped nook, every misplaced volume that hinted at a forgotten researcher's hasty departure. It was during one of his routine explorations, a methodical descent into the forgotten corners of the library's history, that he found it. Tucked away behind a row of crumbling theological treatises, in a section marked 'Esoteric Studies - Restricted Access,' sat a book unlike any other.

It was bound in dark, almost black, leather, so ancient that the surface had become rough and pockmarked, like weathered stone. There was no title on the spine, no author's name, only a faint, almost imperceptible imprint of a stylized, unidentifiable symbol. Curiosity, a rare but potent emotion for Adam, sparked within him. He carefully extracted the volume, its weight surprisingly substantial, its pages brittle and yellowed with age. As he laid it open on a nearby dusty table, the air around him seemed to thicken, as if the very act of disturbing its slumber had awakened something within the room.

The pages were filled with a dense, elegant script, a language that was both familiar and alien, interspersed with intricate, unsettling diagrams. These weren't the simple illustrations found in textbooks; they were complex schematics, depicting flows of energy, interconnectedness of thoughts, and abstract representations of human emotions. And then there were the words. They spoke of influence, of leverage, of the subtle art of bending the will of others without their knowledge. They laid bare the mechanics of human psychology with a chillingly detached precision, not as a means of understanding, but as a toolkit for exploitation.

Adam’s breath hitched. This wasn't merely a book; it was a revelation. It was a blueprint, a detailed, step-by-step guide to the very power he had always craved but never known how to grasp. The manual, as he began to think of it, presented psychological manipulation not as a moral failing, but as an intellectual discipline, a science to be mastered. It spoke of "anchoring," of "reframing," of "emotional contagion," all presented with a cold, calculated logic that resonated deeply with Adam's own analytical mind. He read of strategies to identify vulnerabilities, to exploit insecurities, to systematically dismantle a person’s self-perception until they were putty in the hands of the manipulator. The diagrams illustrated how to plant seeds of doubt, how to subtly redirect conversations, how to create an atmosphere of unease that would erode a person's confidence.

For a man who had spent his life feeling invisible, inadequate, the manual was a key unlocking a door he never knew existed. It was a revelation, a stark contrast to the quiet desperation that had defined his existence. The intellectual superiority he had cultivated as a defense mechanism now found a tangible, exhilarating outlet. The feeling of inadequacy, that gnawing worm of self-doubt, began to recede, replaced by a burgeoning sense of power, an intoxicating awareness of the potential he now held. He saw the library not just as a repository of books, but as a microcosm, a testing ground. The patrons, his colleagues, even the stern faced librarians who patrolled the aisles – they were no longer just people, but subjects, potential pawns in a game he was just beginning to understand. The dusty, forgotten corner of the library had become the cradle of a monstrous transformation. The manual was not just a book; it was an awakening. It was the lure of the unseen, finally made manifest in his trembling hands.

The weeks that followed were a blur of clandestine study. Adam devoured the manual, his reclusive nature now serving as an advantage. He spent his lunch breaks hunched over its pages in a secluded corner of the archives, his evenings dedicated to deciphering its cryptic passages in the dim light of his solitary apartment. The intellectual curiosity that had once been his shield now morphed into a dangerous obsession. He began to see the world through the manual's lens, dissecting every interaction, every flicker of emotion, every subtle nuance of human behavior.

The book was divided into sections, each detailing a specific facet of psychological manipulation. There was 'The Architecture of Perception,' which explained how to subtly alter an individual's understanding of reality through carefully curated information and suggestive language. 'The Symphony of Emotion' delved into the art of eliciting specific feelings – fear, anger, confusion, dependence – and orchestrating them like a conductor leading an orchestra. 'The Subtle Severance' explored techniques for isolating individuals from their support systems, for turning allies into adversaries and eroding trust with surgical precision.

Adam found himself not just reading these concepts, but internalizing them, visualizing them. He imagined himself as a sculptor, his tools not chisels and mallets, but words and gestures. The manual described how to identify a person's deepest insecurities, their unspoken fears, their hidden desires. It detailed how to mirror their language, their body posture, creating an instant, almost subconscious, bond. Then, once trust was established, it showed how to twist these very foundations, to subtly introduce doubt, to reframe past events in a more sinister light, to make the victim question their own sanity.

His growing narcissism was fueled by this newfound understanding. He no longer saw himself as a victim of circumstance, an overlooked nobody. Instead, he began to see himself as a puppeteer, a master strategist observing the intricate dance of human folly from a position of superior intellect. The manual validated his inherent feelings of superiority, transforming them from a defensive mechanism into a source of pride. He wasn't just smart; he was *powerful*. He could manipulate the very fabric of people's minds, shape their realities, control their destinies. The thought sent a thrill through him, a potent cocktail of exhilaration and dark satisfaction. He began to recognize the patterns of manipulation in the world around him, the subtle nudges and suggestions employed by politicians, advertisers, and even everyday acquaintances. But now, he saw it not as a random occurrence, but as a deliberate, systematic process, a science he could not only understand but master.

The library, once his sanctuary, now felt like a training ground. He started to observe his colleagues with a new, calculating gaze. Agnes, the perpetually flustered circulation desk assistant, with her deep-seated fear of making mistakes. Mr. Henderson, the head librarian, whose public persona of geniality masked a brittle ego and a deep-seated insecurity about his own intellectual capabilities. Even the younger interns, eager to please and easily intimidated, presented fascinating case studies.

Adam's initial experiments were tentative, almost accidental, but informed by the manual's principles. He started small, testing the waters of his newfound knowledge. One afternoon, Agnes misplaced a set of overdue notices. Adam, who had discreetly "found" them earlier and placed them on a different trolley, watched as she frantically searched. When she finally found them, a look of bewildered relief washed over her face. Adam approached, a sympathetic smile playing on his lips. "Oh, there they are," he said, his voice gentle. "I thought I saw them over there earlier, but perhaps my eyes were playing tricks. It's been a long day, hasn't it?" He watched as a flicker of confusion crossed Agnes's face, followed by a subtle shift in her posture, a slight slump as if accepting a small, unarticulated burden. He had planted a seed, a tiny seed of doubt about her own perception, about her own memory. He had subtly reframed the situation, making her relief tinged with a sliver of self-recrimination. It was a small victory, barely perceptible, but to Adam, it was a profound confirmation.

He began to subtly alter conversations, guiding them towards topics that played on his colleagues' insecurities. He would casually mention a recent academic paper, feigning admiration, then subtly point out a perceived flaw in the methodology, a logical inconsistency. He watched their reactions closely – the slight frowns, the hesitant nods, the subtle shifts in their gaze. He learned to inject a carefully chosen word, a precisely timed silence, a seemingly innocent question that would send their thoughts spiraling in a direction he had intended. He observed how a simple phrase, "Are you sure about that?" delivered with a certain inflection, could erode confidence. He discovered the power of feigned empathy, mirroring their frustrations, only to subtly suggest that perhaps their own actions or judgments were contributing to their problems.

The library, with its inherent quiet and predictable routines, became his laboratory. He found a peculiar thrill in these small acts of manipulation, a silent testament to the manual's efficacy. Each successful nudge, each planted seed of doubt, was a brushstroke on his canvas of control. He wasn't trying to cause harm, not yet. He was simply testing the mechanics, observing the intricate gears of the human mind, marveling at how easily they could be influenced. The dusty quiet of the stacks became the backdrop for his nascent reign as a psychological puppeteer, each subtle victory a whisper of the darker games to come. The thrill was intoxicating, a stark departure from the dull ache of his previous existence, and it whispered promises of a power he was only beginning to comprehend.

The thrill of subtle manipulation, however, proved to be a fleeting mistress. Adam's experiments, initially confined to planting seeds of doubt and orchestrating minor social discomforts, began to escalate. The detached fascination he felt watching his colleagues falter gave way to a more visceral enjoyment. He craved a stronger reaction, a more profound demonstration of his growing power. The manual, a silent instigator, offered pathways to more potent forms of psychological torment.

He turned his attention to a young, ambitious intern named Leo, who was known for his eagerness to please and his nervous disposition. Adam observed Leo's interactions, noting his desperate need for approval from Mr. Henderson. Adam began a subtle campaign, subtly undermining Leo's confidence in his work. He would offer unsolicited advice, phrased as helpful suggestions, but laced with veiled criticisms. "That's an interesting approach, Leo," he'd say, his tone thoughtfully pensive. "Have you considered how it might be perceived by the Acquisitions Committee? They can be rather... traditional, you know. A slight misstep here could be quite damaging to your reputation, early in your career."

He then escalated, fabricating minor incidents that would cause Leo undue stress. A misplaced file that Adam himself had moved, leading to a frantic search and a mild reprimand from Mr. Henderson, which Adam then "comforted" Leo about, subtly implying Leo's inherent disorganization was the root cause. He began to twist Leo's own words, reinterpreting his enthusiastic contributions in meetings as evidence of overconfidence or a lack of attention to detail. He would engage Leo in long, rambling conversations, ostensibly about library science, but subtly steering the discourse towards hypotheticals involving professional sabotage and the catastrophic consequences of even minor errors.

Adam watched Leo's transformation with a detached, almost clinical, fascination. The intern's usual bright demeanor began to dim. He became visibly anxious, his hands trembling as he sorted books, his eyes darting nervously towards Adam, as if seeking reassurance while simultaneously fearing his judgment. Leo started to second-guess every decision, to apologize excessively for minor tasks, to withdraw from social interactions with colleagues, fearing he might say or do something wrong. Adam felt a prickle of something akin to satisfaction, a low hum of power coursing through him. This was more potent than planting seeds of doubt; this was actively cultivating fear.

One particularly chilling evening, Adam orchestrated a more elaborate scenario. He knew Leo was working late to finish a crucial cataloging project, a task that would impress Mr. Henderson. Adam waited until the library was nearly deserted, the only sounds the hum of the ventilation system and the distant rumble of traffic. He then subtly manipulated the building's security system, triggering a brief, localized power outage in Leo's section of the archives. Emergency lights flickered on, casting long, distorted shadows, and a low, unsettling alarm chirped erratically before silencing itself.

Adam, positioned in a nearby alcove, watched Leo's reaction. The intern jumped, a sharp gasp escaping his lips. He fumbled for his phone, his hands shaking visibly. Adam then made his presence known, stepping out of the shadows with a calm, unhurried pace. "Everything alright, Leo?" he asked, his voice deliberately soft, yet carrying an unnerving resonance in the sudden quiet.

Leo visibly flinched. "A... a power surge, I think," he stammered, his voice tight with an anxiety Adam had meticulously cultivated.

"Hm," Adam mused, his gaze sweeping over the dimly lit aisle. "Happens sometimes in older buildings. Especially when certain systems are under strain. Makes you wonder, doesn't it? About the integrity of the infrastructure. About whether things are as secure as we believe them to be." He let the implication hang in the air, a phantom threat woven from the darkness and the flickering emergency lights. He saw Leo's pupils dilate, his breathing quicken. The manual had taught him that fear was a powerful lever, and the fear of the unknown, of the unseen forces that could disrupt one's carefully constructed reality, was perhaps the most potent of all.

Adam didn't need to say more. He simply offered Leo a thin, knowing smile, a silent acknowledgement of the disquiet he had sown. He watched as Leo, visibly shaken, packed his belongings with hurried, clumsy movements, abandoning the project for the night. Adam remained in the archives long after Leo had fled, the dark leather manual clasped in his hands. The detached fascination was gone, replaced by a burgeoning, almost intoxicating, sense of his own capacity for cruelty. The manual's influence was no longer just intellectual; it was visceral. It was a dangerous, addictive power that was beginning to warp his empathy, to erode his ethical boundaries, drawing him deeper into its dark, compelling allure. The quiet librarian was awakening to a far more terrifying self.

As Adam Tapper delved deeper into the clandestine world revealed by the ancient manual, his clandestine 'games' evolved from subtle psychological nudges to elaborate orchestrated scenarios designed to inflict genuine distress. The library's hushed aisles, once a haven of quiet contemplation, had transformed into his personal theatre of manipulation, and the patrons, once mere background characters, were now unwitting participants in his escalating descent. His initial thrill of intellectual superiority had begun to morph into something far more sinister – a hunger for the raw, visceral reaction of fear, a dark addiction to the tangible evidence of his growing power.

His focus shifted towards individuals he perceived as possessing a certain resilience, a perceived strength that made their eventual unraveling all the more satisfying. It was a perverse form of intellectual challenge, a desire to prove that no one was truly impervious to his meticulously crafted machinations. He would spend weeks observing, gathering intelligence, meticulously cataloging not just books, but the intricate vulnerabilities of the human beings who frequented the library. He studied their routines, their conversations, the subtle tells in their body language that betrayed their deepest insecurities and anxieties. He learned to recognize the tell-tale signs of stress, of loneliness, of unspoken regrets, and he stored this information away, a predator hoarding the scent of his prey.

One particular target emerged: a confident, articulate history professor, Dr. Eleanor Vance. Dr. Vance was a regular at the library, a woman who exuded an aura of calm authority and intellectual prowess. She was well-respected, known for her sharp wit and her unwavering conviction. To Adam, she represented the ultimate challenge, a pillar of intellectual stability he was determined to topple. He began his campaign subtly. He would engage her in brief conversations, always initiated by him, feigning a shared interest in obscure historical texts. He would listen intently, mirroring her language, validating her opinions, all the while subtly gathering ammunition. He noted her occasional sigh when discussing the lack of funding for humanities, her dismissive remarks about sensationalized historical accounts, and her quiet pride in her groundbreaking research.

Using the principles outlined in the manual, Adam began to plant seeds of doubt, not about her work directly, but about the very foundations of her confidence. He would "accidentally" leave relevant articles for her, articles that subtly contradicted her published theories, or presented alternative interpretations that cast her work in a less favorable light. He would then engage her in discussion, feigning ignorance, posing questions that highlighted perceived inconsistencies, always framing them as genuine intellectual curiosity. "Dr. Vance," he'd say, his voice laced with manufactured deference, "I came across this rather peculiar article. It suggests a completely different interpretation of the Peloponnesian War's naval strategies. I was wondering your thoughts? It seems to directly challenge some of the established narratives, even... some of the ones you've so eloquently presented."

He also began to subtly undermine her interactions with others within the library. He'd make seemingly innocuous comments to her colleagues about Dr. Vance's "unusual intensity" lately, or her "rather assertive" demeanor, framing it as concern for her well-being while subtly casting her in a negative light. He'd intercept casual greetings, offering a slightly too-prolonged, unsettling stare that would leave the recipient questioning its meaning. He engineered situations where Dr. Vance might feel misunderstood or subtly undermined. He would "accidentally" misfile a critical research paper she had requested, forcing her to spend hours searching, his apology delivered with a subtle hint that perhaps she hadn't been clear enough in her request, thus questioning her communication skills.

The manual detailed specific tactics for inducing paranoia, and Adam applied them with chilling precision. He learned that creating a sense of being watched, of being judged, could be incredibly effective. He would often be present, a silent observer, whenever Dr. Vance was engrossed in her work, his presence a constant, unnerving weight. He would deliberately drop a book with a loud thud when she was concentrating, or cough softly from a nearby aisle, creating a subtle but persistent disturbance. He observed her growing discomfort – the way her shoulders tensed, the slight tremor in her hands as she reached for her pen, the way her gaze would flick nervously towards his hidden location.

He witnessed the first tangible cracks appear in her composure. Her lectures, once delivered with effortless grace, became punctuated by hesitant pauses. Her interactions with library staff became shorter, more guarded. She started to exhibit a subtle paranoia, frequently looking over her shoulder, double-checking the placement of her belongings, a stark contrast to her previous confident self-assurance. Adam felt a surge of exhilaration, a dark satisfaction that was far more potent than any intellectual validation he had ever received. He was not just understanding the manual; he was living it, breathing it, becoming it. The quiet librarian was no longer content with merely observing the world; he was actively shaping it, one carefully orchestrated moment of fear at a time. The lure of the unseen had become an irresistible, destructive force, and the shadows it cast were lengthening ominously.

The library's quiet hum, once a comforting lullaby, now vibrated with an undercurrent of unease, a subtle discordance that Adam Tapper had meticulously composed. His carefully orchestrated 'games' were no longer confined to the dusty archives; they were bleeding into the fabric of everyday life, leaving a trail of disquiet. The manual, clutched tightly in his hand, felt less like a collection of arcane knowledge and more like a living entity, whispering insidious suggestions, guiding his hand towards ever darker designs.

He observed the subtle shifts in his chosen victims with a detached, almost clinical satisfaction. He saw the growing anxiety in their eyes, the hesitant tremor in their voices, the subtle ways their interactions with others frayed at the edges. It was a perverse validation, proof that the intricate theories laid out in the brittle pages of the leather-bound tome were not mere academic exercises but potent tools for reshaping human reality.

His latest target was a seemingly ordinary man, a middle-aged accountant named Mr. Davies, who frequented the library's business section. Davies, with his predictable routine and quiet demeanor, presented an ideal canvas. Adam had noticed Davies's subtle reliance on routine, his almost compulsive need for order, and a faint undercurrent of loneliness that seemed to permeate his solitary existence. These were the cracks Adam sought, the fissures through which he could introduce the corrosive acid of doubt and paranoia.

Adam's initial approach was disarmingly simple. He began to "accidentally" encounter Davies in the business section, always offering a polite nod, a brief, innocuous comment about the weather or a current event. He subtly mirrored Davies's language, his posture, creating an almost imperceptible sense of familiarity. Then, he began to introduce minor disruptions to Davies's meticulously ordered world. He'd subtly alter the arrangement of books on a shelf Davies frequently used, or move a commonly placed newspaper a few inches from its usual spot. He would then observe Davies's subtle reaction – a furrowed brow, a brief pause, a moment of disorientation.

The manual, however, offered avenues beyond mere trivial annoyances. Adam moved to more calculated maneuvers, designed to sow discord and isolation. He learned of Davies's strained relationship with his adult son, a communication breakdown stemming from years of unspoken resentments. Adam seized upon this vulnerability. Through carefully worded, anonymous emails sent from a disposable account, Adam began to insinuate himself into this existing rift. He would fabricate conversations, subtly twisting Davies's own words and concerns into accusations of neglect and criticism directed at his son. He'd then subtly pass on fabricated "concerns" from the son back to Davies, carefully framing them as worried observations about his father's supposed erratic behavior.

"I overheard your son mentioning how worried he is about you, Mr. Davies," Adam casually remarked one afternoon, his voice laced with feigned concern. "He said you seemed... distracted lately. Perhaps a bit forgetful. He worries about you being alone." Adam watched as Davies's face paled, his eyes widening with a mixture of fear and confusion. The seed of doubt had been planted, not just about his own mind, but about the very loyalty of his estranged son.

Adam's strategy of isolation intensified. He noticed Davies's only close friend was a fellow accountant, a man named Peterson, with whom he played chess every Thursday. Adam subtly orchestrated a series of "misunderstandings" between them. He anonymously sent Peterson a fabricated message, supposedly from Davies, canceling their chess game at the last minute with a curt, uncharacteristic excuse. Then, he sent Davies a subtly altered version of a message from Peterson, implying Peterson was cancelling due to a prior engagement, laced with a hint of impatience. The result was a growing chasm of silence between the two friends, leaving Davies increasingly isolated, his world shrinking with each passing day.

The culmination of this phase was a deliberate act designed to induce severe paranoia. Adam learned that Davies was meticulous about his finances, his desk at work a shrine to organized ledgers and meticulously filed invoices. Adam, through a discreet act of insider access facilitated by a disgruntled junior library staffer he'd been subtly manipulating for weeks, managed to gain access to Davies's office. He didn't steal anything; that wasn't the point. Instead, he subtly altered a few key figures in Davies's financial statements, small discrepancies, almost imperceptible, but enough to trigger a deep-seated fear of error and exposure in the meticulous accountant. He also rearranged a few items on Davies's desk, a subtle disruption of the sacred order.

When Davies returned to work the next day, the impact was immediate. Adam, observing from a vantage point that allowed him to witness the subtle ripple effects within the library's community, saw the accountant's usual calm façade shatter. Davies's face contorted in panic as he reviewed his spreadsheets. He began frantically checking and rechecking his figures, his breath coming in short, sharp gasps. He then noticed the subtly rearranged items on his desk, his eyes wide with dawning horror. To Adam, the scene was a masterpiece. He saw Davies's carefully constructed world, his sense of order and control, crumbling before his eyes. The accountant's frantic movements, his palpable anxiety, the dawning realization that his reality was no longer stable – it was precisely the visceral reaction Adam had craved.

The manual had foretold this: "When the edifice of their perceived reality begins to fracture, the observer will feel the ground shift beneath them. Their certainty will erode, replaced by a gnawing dread, a suspicion that unseen forces are at play. This is the point of maximum leverage, where their will becomes most pliable." Adam felt a dark exultation bloom within him. He was no longer just a librarian; he was a force, a disrupter of worlds, a silent architect of chaos. The manual's dark promise was being fulfilled, and the librarian, once cloaked in the anonymity of his quiet life, was emerging from the shadows, a harbinger of a terror he was only beginning to unleash. The whisper of fear he had sown in Mr. Davies was growing into a deafening roar, and Adam Tapper was listening, a chilling smile playing on his lips.

The leather-bound manual lay open on Adam's lap, its ancient pages a stark contrast to the sterile, fluorescent-lit environment of the library's sub-basement. He traced the elegant, unsettling script with a fingertip, the words weaving a complex tapestry of the human psyche. This was not a book for casual reading; it was a dissection, a cold, clinical exposé of the invisible threads that bound human beings together, and how those threads could be manipulated, frayed, or even snapped.

He immersed himself in the chapter titled 'The Architecture of Perception.' It spoke of how reality itself was a malleable construct, shaped not by objective truth, but by the information individuals received and how it was framed. Adam read of "anchoring," the technique of establishing a baseline of perception, and then subtly shifting it to create a desired outcome. The manual explained how to present information in a specific order, how to strategically withhold or emphasize certain details, and how to utilize loaded language to pre-dispose an individual's thoughts. It was less about outright deception and more about curated truth, a subtle art of leading a person to a preconceived conclusion without them realizing they were being guided. Adam visualized it: a sculptor carefully chipping away at a block of marble, revealing not the statue's inherent form, but the one the sculptor envisioned. The library, with its endless stream of patrons seeking information, suddenly appeared not as a sanctuary of knowledge, but as a vast, untapped reservoir of minds ripe for subtle redirection.

Next, he delved into 'The Symphony of Emotion.' This section was even more intoxicating. It detailed how to identify the dominant emotional states of an individual – fear, anger, joy, sadness, anxiety – and then, through carefully calibrated stimuli, amplify or suppress them. The manual described "emotional contagion," the phenomenon of emotions spreading through groups, and how one could initiate and control this spread. Adam's mind conjured images of a conductor leading an orchestra, not with instruments, but with words, gestures, and even silences. He pictured himself, not with a baton, but with a glint in his eye and a precisely chosen phrase, capable of orchestrating a cascade of fear or a wave of desperate hope. The manual explained how to identify triggers, how to exploit existing emotional states, and how to create new ones. It spoke of "reframing," taking a negative experience and reinterpreting it in a way that fostered dependence or gratitude towards the manipulator. Adam felt a shiver of dark fascination. He had always been an observer of human emotion, a detached analyst of the subtle shifts in facial expressions and body language. Now, he saw those observations not as mere curiosities, but as data points, as keys to unlocking a deeper, more potent form of influence.

The concept of "leverage" permeated every section. It wasn't about brute force or overt threats. It was about identifying a person's core needs, their deepest insecurities, their unspoken desires, and then using those as a fulcrum. The manual detailed how to uncover these vulnerabilities – through careful listening, through probing questions disguised as casual conversation, through analyzing their written words, their choices, their interactions. Adam began to see his own life, his perceived inadequacies, his yearning for recognition, not as personal failings, but as potential sources of his own leverage, should the need arise. But that was a thought for another time. His focus was outward, on the unsuspecting world.

He felt a distinct shift within himself. The gnawing worm of inadequacy, the constant companion of his solitary existence, began to recede. It was being replaced by something new, something exhilarating. It was the intoxicating bloom of narcissism, not the flamboyant, attention-seeking kind, but a quiet, internal validation. He no longer saw himself as the overlooked librarian, the spectral presence haunting the stacks. He saw himself as a strategist, a puppeteer in the making. The manual provided the blueprint, the intricate schematics of the human mind. His own analytical intellect, once a shield against his insecurities, was now the perfect tool to wield this knowledge. He began to perceive the library not as a place of quiet refuge, but as a testing ground, a meticulously controlled environment where he could hone his nascent skills. His colleagues, the patrons, even the stern librarians who patrolled the aisles – they were no longer just people. They were subjects, variables in a complex equation he was learning to solve.

He started to visualize practical applications, even if only in his mind. He imagined a conversation with Agnes, the perpetually flustered circulation desk assistant. The manual spoke of identifying a person's need for validation. Agnes often fumbled with the checkout system, her fear of making mistakes palpable. Adam pictured himself approaching her after a minor error, not with a reprimand, but with a gentle, reassuring tone. "Don't worry, Agnes," he'd say, his voice soft and understanding. "It happens to everyone. Especially with these new systems. They're quite complicated, aren't they? You're doing a wonderful job under a lot of pressure." He saw her shoulders relax, a flicker of relief crossing her face, followed by a subtle gratitude that he had perceived her struggle. It was a small, almost insignificant interaction, but in his mind, it was a demonstration of control, a subtle shift in Agnes's emotional state, all orchestrated by him.

He turned his attention to Mr. Henderson, the head librarian. Henderson's outward joviality masked a brittle ego, a constant need to be seen as competent and knowledgeable. Adam recalled Henderson's recent struggle to understand a new digital archiving software. The manual discussed exploiting pride and the fear of appearing ignorant. Adam envisioned approaching Henderson, not with answers, but with carefully phrased questions, feigning a minor confusion about the software himself, thereby subtly flattering Henderson into explaining it, positioning him as the expert. "Mr. Henderson," he'd begin, his brow furrowed in simulated perplexity, "I'm having a bit of trouble with this new archive interface. It seems quite intricate. I was hoping you might shed some light on how you navigate its more complex functions? Your understanding of these systems is always so... thorough." He saw Henderson puff up, a subtle smile playing on his lips as he readily launched into an explanation, his ego temporarily soothed, his own insecurities momentarily forgotten as he bask in Adam's manufactured admiration.

The theoretical knowledge began to crystallize, forming a tangible hunger for practical application. It wasn't about malice, not yet. It was about the sheer, unadulterated thrill of understanding, of mastery. The manual was a map to a hidden world, a world of influence and control that lay just beneath the surface of everyday interactions. And Adam, the quiet, overlooked librarian, was discovering he had the key. He found himself dissecting every casual conversation, every fleeting glance, every subtle social cue, not for their inherent meaning, but for the potential leverage they offered. The library, once a refuge from the complexities of human interaction, was transforming into his personal laboratory, a silent testament to the power of the unseen. The manual wasn't just a book; it was a catalyst, igniting a dormant, dangerous curiosity within him, a nascent desire to not just understand the mechanics of control, but to wield them. The whisper of his own potential, amplified by the ancient text, was becoming a siren song, pulling him deeper into the allure of the unseen.

The dust motes danced in the shafts of sunlight that pierced the gloom of the library's less-trafficked sections, oblivious to the seismic shift occurring within Adam's mind. He moved through the hushed aisles, no longer just a custodian of books, but a nascent architect of perceptions. The manual, tucked discreetly into his satchel, was a constant, pulsing presence, its theories now demanding empirical validation. He was eager, not for malice, but for the intoxicating confirmation that the labyrinthine pathways of the human mind were, indeed, navigable, and more importantly, steerable.

His first target was Agnes, the perpetually flustered woman at the circulation desk. The manual had spoken of 'anchoring,' of establishing a baseline and then subtly shifting it. Agnes's baseline, Adam had observed, was a low hum of anxiety, a fear of inefficiency that often manifested as nervous fumbling with the barcode scanner. Today, she was wrestling with a particularly stubborn patron, a gentleman who seemed to delight in the slow, deliberate unfolding of his overdue book return. Adam watched from a distance, a detached observer at the edge of a stage. Agnes's brow was furrowed, her movements jerky with suppressed frustration.

When the patron finally departed, leaving Agnes sighing with relief, Adam chose his moment. He approached the desk, not with the usual polite nod, but with a carefully calibrated expression of concern. "Agnes," he began, his voice pitched low, a gentle murmur designed to be both sympathetic and slightly unsettling. "Are you quite alright? You seemed... distressed a moment ago."

Agnes blinked, her hands instinctively smoothing her apron. "Oh, it's nothing, Adam. Just a difficult patron, that's all."

"Difficult?" Adam leaned in slightly, lowering his voice further. "It looked more than difficult. It looked... overwhelming. Are you sure you're not feeling too much pressure? I noticed how your hands were shaking when you were scanning that last book."

Her hands stopped their smoothing. She glanced down at them, a flicker of alarm in her eyes. “Shaking? No, I don’t think so.”

“Oh, they were,” Adam insisted, his tone unwavering, yet laced with a subtle, almost paternal reassurance. “It was quite noticeable. Especially when you were trying to get that code to register. Almost like you were… scared of making a mistake. Are you sure you’re getting enough support here, Agnes? It’s a demanding job, and sometimes, when things get tough, people can feel… isolated.”

He saw it then – the subtle widening of her eyes, the almost imperceptible tremor that ran through her. He had planted the seed. He hadn’t lied, not entirely. He had merely emphasized a perceived tremor, amplified a fleeting anxiety into something tangible, something she could almost feel herself. He had anchored her perception to her own supposed distress.

“I… I don’t know,” she stammered, her voice losing some of its usual crispness. “Maybe… maybe I am a bit stressed. It has been a busy week.”

Adam offered a small, knowing smile. “It’s understandable. Don’t let it get to you. Just… try to breathe. Take it one patron at a time. You’re doing your best.” He withdrew, leaving her with a new, carefully constructed layer of self-doubt, a whisper of an unease that hadn't been there moments before. He felt a quiet surge of triumph, a spark of recognition. The manual worked. The theoretical was becoming the tangible.

Later that week, he turned his attention to Mr. Peterson, a regular patron known for his meticulous adherence to library rules and his somewhat condescending air. Peterson had a habit of leaving his returned books with their spines precisely aligned, a silent judgment on the perceived sloppiness of others. Adam observed Peterson returning a stack of novels, placing them with his characteristic precision.

Adam waited until Peterson had moved towards the exit, then casually picked up one of the books. He opened it to a random page, then subtly bent the corner of a page inwards, just a fraction, before placing the book back on the returns cart, slightly askew from its companions. It was a minuscule act of disruption, almost invisible.

A few minutes later, as Peterson was pausing to retrieve a forgotten umbrella near the entrance, Adam made his move. He approached Peterson with a bemused expression. “Mr. Peterson, I believe you might have accidentally… disturbed one of the books you just returned.”

Peterson turned, his brow furrowing. "Disturbed? What do you mean?"

Adam gestured subtly towards the returns cart. "That copy of 'The Maltese Falcon.' It seems to have acquired a rather unfortunate crease on page eighty-seven. Did you perhaps… lean on it a little too heavily?" He kept his tone light, but there was an undercurrent of gentle, almost polite, accusation. He was testing the waters of Peterson's need for self-perceived order and his aversion to being seen as careless.

Peterson's face tightened. He strode over to the cart, his eyes scanning the spines. He found the book, his hand hovering over the cover. His gaze immediately fixed on the page Adam had indicated. A flicker of annoyance, quickly masked, crossed his features. "A crease? No, that's… impossible. I am always extremely careful." He opened the book, his fingers tracing the bent corner. The subtle rigidity in his posture intensified.

"I'm sure you are," Adam said smoothly, offering a disarming smile. "It's just that when you placed them down, it seemed a little… rushed. Perhaps it happened as you were setting them on the cart? Sometimes, when we're trying to be efficient, we overlook the small details." He was framing Peterson's action not as deliberate carelessness, but as an unavoidable consequence of his own perceived haste, a subtle ego-saving manoeuvre that still pinned the blame on him.

Peterson opened his mouth to protest, then closed it. He smoothed the offending crease with a vigorous motion, his lips pressed into a thin line. He shot Adam a curt nod, a silent acknowledgment of the perceived imperfection, and then practically fled the library. Adam watched him go, a flicker of something akin to intellectual satisfaction warming him. He had gently nudged Peterson's carefully constructed self-image, introduced a microscopic crack. It was a small victory, but it was a victory nonetheless. The manual's principles were not abstract theories; they were practical tools.

His most daring experiment, thus far, involved Sarah, a bright, ambitious intern who often sought Adam's advice on research methodologies. Sarah had a distinct competitive streak, a desire to impress. Adam had overheard her discussing a complex research paper she was writing, a paper she believed would be her ticket to a prestigious postgraduate program. The manual's section on 'planting seeds of doubt' felt particularly relevant.

During a casual conversation by the photocopier, Adam steered the discussion towards her thesis. "Sarah," he began, his tone thoughtful, "I've been thinking about your work on early modern cartography. It's incredibly ambitious."

Sarah beamed. "Thank you, Adam. I'm really excited about it."

"And rightly so," Adam continued, picking up a stack of papers from the copier. "But I was rereading some of Professor Albright's seminal work on the subject just yesterday. He makes a rather... strong case for the limitations of relying solely on textual analysis for that period. He argues that the visual elements, the very *framing* of the maps, often reveal more than the inscriptions themselves. It's quite a compelling argument, really. He suggests that many earlier analyses, including some of the more prominent ones, might have been... somewhat superficial in their interpretation of the visual data."

He watched Sarah's face closely. The initial enthusiasm began to dim, replaced by a subtle unease. He hadn't directly criticized her work, hadn't even mentioned her by name. He had merely introduced a highly respected external authority who, through Adam's carefully chosen words, implicitly cast doubt on the very foundations of her current approach. He had introduced a concept, a possibility of superficiality, and attached it to her area of expertise.

"Superficial?" Sarah echoed, a frown creasing her brow. "But I've spent months cross-referencing texts and visual representations. I thought I was being thorough."

"Oh, you are thorough, Sarah, I have no doubt," Adam reassured her, his voice a balm over the burgeoning wound. "Your dedication is admirable. But Albright's point is more about... the underlying assumptions. He argues that without a deep understanding of the *political and social context* in which these maps were created, any interpretation of their visual elements can be easily skewed. It's a very nuanced point. He brings up an example, a specific map from Amsterdam, where scholars previously assumed it was a straightforward depiction of trade routes, but Albright argues it was actually a coded message about religious dissent. Fascinating, isn't it? Makes you wonder how many other interpretations have been, shall we say, misdirected."

He could see the wheels turning in her mind. The confident gleam in her eyes had been replaced by a flicker of uncertainty. He hadn't attacked her directly, but he had subtly undermined her confidence in her own methodology. He had planted a seed of doubt, a question that would now haunt her research. Was she superficial? Was her interpretation misdirected? The seed would grow, watered by her own ambition and the inherent anxieties of academic pursuit.

He concluded the conversation with a seemingly innocuous comment. "Anyway, just a thought. Professor Albright's work is quite... thought-provoking. Perhaps worth a glance, if you have time." He walked away, leaving Sarah standing by the photocopier, her gaze distant, already lost in a labyrinth of second-guessing.

These were not acts of malice, not yet. They were calculated experiments, meticulously executed. Each interaction was a data point, a confirmation of the manual's efficacy. The thrill wasn't in causing distress, but in the sheer intellectual artistry of it all. He was a conductor, not of an orchestra, but of the subtle currents of human belief and perception. The quiet hum of the library, once a backdrop to his solitary existence, had become the vibrant, pulsing arena for his nascent manipulations. He felt a growing sense of power, a quiet exhilaration that hummed beneath his skin. The manual had unlocked a door, and he was eagerly stepping through, not into darkness, but into a world of his own carefully curated design, where the unseen forces of influence were his to command. The library, in its ordered serenity, was the perfect laboratory, each unsuspecting patron a willing participant in his unfolding mastery. He was learning to dance with the shadows, and the steps were becoming more fluid, more confident, with every whispered word, every planted doubt.

The hum of the library, once a comforting murmur, had begun to thrum with a more potent, almost predatory energy. Adam's earlier experiments, the subtle nudges to Agnes's anxiety, the mild disruption of Mr. Peterson's fastidiousness, and the intellectual seeds of doubt sown in Sarah's ambitious mind, had served their purpose. They were the preliminary calibrations, the gentle warming-up exercises before the true symphony of manipulation began. The manual, a constant weight in his satchel, felt less like a forbidden text and more like an extension of his will, its pages whispering not just theories, but directives. The detached fascination was evolving, shedding its academic cloak for something altogether more visceral. He was no longer merely an observer; he was the architect of unease, the puppeteer pulling invisible strings that tightened around the psyches of those around him.

His gaze fell upon Mrs. Gable, a woman whose quiet life revolved around her prize-winning roses and the predictable rhythm of her book club selections. She was a creature of habit, her presence in the library as regular as the ticking of the grandfather clock in the main hall. Adam had observed her for weeks, noting her gentle demeanor, her soft-spoken inquiries, and the almost apologetic way she returned her books. She was the antithesis of the chaos he was beginning to cultivate, and therefore, the perfect canvas. The manual's chapter on 'cultivating phobias' was a particularly chilling read, detailing how to latch onto existing anxieties and amplify them into paralyzing fears. For Mrs. Gable, Adam had identified a mild aversion to spiders – a common enough fear, often dismissed as trivial. Trivial, he mused, until it was all-consuming.

The plan began with a seemingly innocuous exchange. Mrs. Gable approached the circulation desk, her arms laden with a stack of biographies. Adam, stationed nearby, ostensibly reshelving, caught her eye and offered a polite smile. “Good afternoon, Mrs. Gable. Finding some good reads today?”

She returned his smile, a soft, crinkling of the eyes. “Oh, yes, Adam. Just finished the latest from Elizabeth Ashton. Utterly charming.” She placed her books on the counter. As she did, Adam subtly reached into his satchel and retrieved a small, transparent plastic bag. Inside, a dark, spindly spider, no larger than his thumbnail, scuttled restlessly. He had acquired it from a secluded corner of the library’s overgrown back garden, a place rarely disturbed. With a practiced, almost imperceptible movement, he allowed the bag to slip from his grasp as he shifted his weight. It landed with a soft *thump* near Mrs. Gable’s elbow, partially concealed beneath the edge of a discarded newspaper.

“Oh, my!” Mrs. Gable exclaimed, her voice a soft gasp. She noticed the bag immediately, her eyes drawn to the frantic movement within. “What’s this?”

Adam feigned surprise, his own gaze following hers. “Good heavens, I don’t know. It must have fallen.” He made a show of reaching for it, his movements deliberately slow. As his fingers neared the bag, he paused, his eyes widening slightly. “Is that… a spider?” His voice was laced with a carefully manufactured unease.

Mrs. Gable’s smile vanished. Her hand, which had been resting on a book, froze. Her breath hitched. “A spider?” she whispered, her voice barely audible.

“Yes,” Adam confirmed, his tone shifting from surprise to a more pronounced apprehension. “A rather… active one, wouldn’t you say?” He nudged the bag slightly with his finger, causing the spider to dart across the plastic.

Mrs. Gable recoiled, a visible tremor running through her. Her eyes, usually so calm and kind, were wide with a dawning alarm. “Oh, dear,” she murmured, her hand flying to her chest. “I… I really don’t like spiders.”

“No, I can see that,” Adam said, his voice softening into a tone of sympathetic concern, though his eyes were alight with a cold, detached curiosity. “It’s quite a large one, isn't it? And it looks... rather hairy. Sometimes, those ones can be quite nasty." He was layering the fear, imbuing the harmless arachnid with an exaggerated menace. He remembered the manual's advice: '*Amplify the perceived threat. Emphasize physical characteristics associated with danger. Introduce ambiguity regarding the species to allow the mind to conjure its worst fears.*'

He watched as Mrs. Gable's breathing became shallow and rapid. She was trying to appear composed, but the subtle clenching of her jaw, the slight sheen of perspiration on her upper lip, betrayed her growing panic. He then employed another technique from the manual: 'associative suggestion.'

"You know," he began, his voice conversational, almost as an aside, "I was reading the other day about a rather unfortunate incident... a woman in the next town over. She found a spider, not unlike this one, in her teacup. She didn't notice it until she'd taken a sip. Apparently, it had a rather nasty bite, and she was ill for weeks. Quite distressing." He paused, letting the implication hang in the air. He hadn't seen any such incident, of course. It was a fabrication, a carefully crafted story designed to link the spider to a tangible, negative consequence.

Mrs. Gable's eyes darted from the bag to Adam, then back again. Her face had gone pale. "In her... teacup?" she stammered, the very idea seemingly too much to bear.

"Yes," Adam confirmed, his gaze now fixed on her reaction, his own internal alarm bells ringing with a different kind of excitation. He was seeing the fear manifest, the carefully constructed facade of her composure begin to crumble. "It's remarkable how something so small can cause such... disruption. Especially for those who are particularly sensitive to them." He was subtly suggesting that she was, indeed, sensitive, validating her fear and encouraging its escalation.

He saw a faint, almost imperceptible movement at the edge of Mrs. Gable's vision. A shadow, perhaps, cast by the flickering fluorescent lights, or a stray strand of her own hair. But in her heightened state of anxiety, amplified by Adam's carefully chosen words, her mind latched onto it. Her eyes widened, her pupils dilating. She let out a small, choked cry, stumbling back from the counter, her books scattering across the floor.

"It's... it's moving!" she gasped, pointing a trembling finger towards an empty space on the floor. "It's out of the bag! It's coming towards me!"

Adam followed her gaze, his own expression one of mild alarm. “Where? I don’t see anything, Mrs. Gable.” He knew, of course, that there was nothing there. The spider was still safely contained within the plastic bag, oblivious to the turmoil it had unleashed. But the illusion was powerful, a testament to the malleability of perception. Her fear had created a phantom, a manifestation of her own internal terror.

A librarian from across the room, alerted by Mrs. Gable’s cry, rushed over. “Is everything alright, Mrs. Gable?”

Mrs. Gable, however, was beyond rational explanation. She was hyperventilating, her hands clasped over her mouth, her eyes wide with unshed tears, scanning the floor frantically. “A spider,” she managed to choke out. “It... it escaped. It was enormous!”

Adam, with a sigh of feigned concern, calmly picked up the plastic bag. “Here it is, Mrs. Gable,” he said, holding it up. “Still safe and sound. Perhaps you just... thought you saw it move?” He kept his tone gentle, suggesting that her perception might have been unreliable, a common occurrence when one was frightened. He watched as she looked at the bag, then at the empty floor, her brow furrowed with confusion and residual terror. The seeds of doubt about her own senses were now sown.

The librarian, a kind older woman named Brenda, quickly gathered Mrs. Gable’s fallen books. “There, there, dear. It was just a little spider. Nothing to be frightened of.”

But it was too late. The carefully orchestrated scenario had worked. Mrs. Gable, visibly shaken, declined further assistance and practically fled the library, her face etched with a profound disquiet. Adam watched her go, a peculiar sensation blooming in his chest. It wasn’t just intellectual satisfaction anymore. It was a heady rush, a sense of potent power that coursed through his veins. He had seen fear bloom, had witnessed the rapid, almost instantaneous dismantling of a calm mind, and the experience was... exhilarating. The manual was more than a guide; it was a catalyst, transforming his quiet curiosity into something far more potent, far more consuming.

Later that week, Adam set his sights on a more challenging target: Mr. Henderson, a gruff, no-nonsense retired detective who frequented the library’s history section. Henderson was a man who prided himself on his sharp intellect and his unwavering skepticism. He was the kind of person who would likely dismiss any attempt at manipulation as absurd. But the manual offered a chapter specifically on ‘undermining certainty,’ focusing on creating an environment of pervasive doubt that would even infect the most resolute minds.

Adam's approach was different this time. It wasn't about planting a seed of fear, but about cultivating an atmosphere of subtle, pervasive paranoia. He began by altering Henderson's routine. Henderson always returned his books on Tuesdays, and always placed them on the cart by the history section. Adam, however, made sure that on this particular Tuesday, a few of Henderson's returned books were subtly misplaced. Not lost, but moved to a different shelf, a different section, just far enough to be out of place, but close enough to be found with a little searching.

He observed Henderson's arrival. The man walked with a purposeful stride, his eyes scanning the shelves with practiced efficiency. He approached the returns cart, his brow furrowed slightly as he noticed the absence of his usual stack. Adam, loitering nearby, pretending to read a newspaper, watched as Henderson began his search. He moved through the aisles, his movements becoming more agitated with each passing minute.

When Henderson finally found one of his books, tucked away on a shelf dedicated to maritime history, he let out a low growl. He approached Adam, his expression thunderous. "Did you see someone moving my books, son?"

Adam lowered his newspaper, his face a mask of innocent surprise. "Your books, Mr. Henderson? I haven't seen anyone moving them. They're usually right here on the cart."

Henderson grunted, his suspicion clearly unassuaded. "Someone's messing with me. I don't like it." He continued his search, and Adam ensured that another two of his books were similarly relocated.

The next day, Adam escalated the game. He observed Henderson engrossed in a thick volume on the Napoleonic Wars. Adam then approached the table, a slight frown on his face. He picked up a nearby journal, one that Henderson had evidently been referencing. He then casually, almost accidentally, brushed against the table, causing a small cascade of loose papers to fall from it.

"Oh, I'm so sorry, Mr. Henderson!" Adam exclaimed, his voice full of contrition. "Clumsy of me."

Henderson glared at the scattered papers, his lips pressed into a thin line. "Just watch where you're going, kid," he muttered, though his eyes held a flicker of something beyond annoyance. He began to gather the papers, his movements brusque.

Adam, however, noticed something else. One of the papers, a page of notes with densely packed handwriting, had landed near his feet. He picked it up, ostensibly to return it. But as he did, he subtly scanned the contents. It was a meticulously organized list of dates, troop movements, and battle strategies – Henderson's research notes. Adam's eyes, however, caught on a small, almost illegible annotation in the margin of one page. It looked like a date, but it was smudged, almost like an ink blot.

He handed the paper back to Henderson, his expression now one of mild concern. "Mr. Henderson, I'm not sure if this is important, but... this annotation here... it looks a bit odd, doesn't it?" He pointed to the smudged mark. "Almost like... someone tried to deliberately obscure something."

Henderson took the paper, his gaze sharpening. He squinted at the annotation. "Obscure what?" His voice was laced with a sudden wariness.

"I don't know," Adam said, his voice lowering conspiratorially. "It's just that, when you have your notes so meticulously organized, it seems unusual to have something so... unclear. Unless, of course, it's intentionally unclear. Perhaps a code? Or maybe... someone tampered with it?" He was planting the idea, the suggestion that Henderson's own meticulousness was being undermined by an unseen force.

Henderson's hand tightened around the paper. His skepticism, usually a formidable shield, seemed to waver. He looked from the annotation to Adam, then back again, a flicker of suspicion crossing his gruff features. He said nothing, but the air around him seemed to thicken with a new, unarticulated unease. He returned to his notes, but his focus was broken. His eyes kept darting to the smudged annotation, his brow perpetually furrowed.

The final touch, the stroke that would truly cement the unease, came later that afternoon. Adam, knowing Henderson often lingered until closing, waited until the library was nearly empty. He then casually approached Henderson's table, holding a copy of the library's daily schedule.

"Mr. Henderson," Adam began, his voice pitched low, "I'm not sure if you're aware, but the library is undergoing some... unscheduled maintenance this week. Apparently, there have been some minor security concerns, and they're doing a sweep of the building. Nothing to worry about, of course, but it means they're checking all the areas, including the... more obscure ones." He let the words hang in the air, imbuing them with an unspoken significance. He was hinting at surveillance, at an intrusion into even the most private of spaces.

Henderson looked up, his eyes narrowed. “Security concerns? What kind of concerns?”

“Oh, I don’t know the specifics,” Adam said, feigning ignorance. “Just... general concerns. Sometimes, when these things happen, they put up extra... monitoring equipment. Just to be safe, you understand.” He gestured vaguely towards the ceiling. “You know, to ensure everything is secure.”

He saw the wheels turning in Henderson’s mind. The misplaced books, the smudged annotation, the talk of security sweeps and monitoring equipment – it was all coalescing into a narrative of subtle intrusion. Henderson, a man who had spent his career hunting for hidden truths and uncovering conspiracies, was now susceptible to the very paranoia he used to instill in others.

Adam left Henderson sitting at his table, his gaze now sweeping the room with a new, hyper-vigilant intensity. He wasn't just reading history anymore; he was becoming a part of a new, unsettling narrative, one that Adam was carefully weaving around him. The raw enjoyment Adam felt was a stark contrast to the intellectual curiosity of his earlier experiments. This was about the tangible impact, the visible tremor in the human psyche, the delicious unraveling of a seemingly solid mind. The manual was not just a tool; it was a drug, and Adam was quickly becoming addicted to its intoxicating effects. The library, once a sanctuary of quiet contemplation, had transformed into his personal playground, and the echoes of fear he was creating were the sweetest music he had ever heard.

The fluorescent lights of the library, once a sterile testament to order, now seemed to cast a more malevolent glow, reflecting the escalating darkness Adam felt unfurling within him. Mrs. Gable’s trembling hands and Mr. Henderson’s suspicious glances were more than mere data points; they were the tangible results of his carefully orchestrated endeavors, the first brushstrokes on a canvas of manufactured chaos. The manual, no longer a theoretical curiosity, had become his gospel, its pages whispering secrets of influence and control that resonated deep within his being. He found himself returning to the same passages, not for instruction, but for a morbid sense of validation, a chilling echo of his own burgeoning capabilities. The detached intellectualism that had initially driven him was rapidly giving way to something far more primal, a heady intoxication derived from the visible fraying of others’ composure.

His gaze drifted towards the far corner of the reading room, where Agnes, perpetually hunched over her research, was meticulously annotating a historical document. The subtle anxieties he had previously nudged her with—a misplaced file, a fleeting shadow that seemed to linger too long—had undoubtedly taken root. He imagined her now, perhaps questioning the integrity of her own memory, her meticulously organized world beginning to feel a little less stable. He hadn't seen her directly since his initial interventions, but he felt her presence, a silent testament to the efficacy of his subtle poisons. He knew the manual's techniques for 'inducing cognitive dissonance' were particularly potent, and he had employed them with a deftness that surprised even himself. Whispers of fabricated errors in her research, strategically placed 'anonymous' notes questioning her sources, and the subtle alteration of her carefully arranged notes had all contributed to a growing sense of self-doubt. It was a slow burn, a gradual erosion of her confidence, designed to leave her questioning not just her work, but her own judgment. He envisioned her late at night, poring over her findings with a frantic intensity, searching for the phantom flaws he had so carefully introduced. The thought sent a thrill, sharp and cold, through him.

Then there was Sarah, the ambitious intern, whose initial eagerness had been subtly tainted with a gnawing suspicion. Adam had noticed her growing apprehension in the way she double-checked her work, the hesitant way she approached her superiors, the increasing frequency with which she scanned her surroundings, as if expecting something—or someone—to betray her. He had planted a seed of doubt about a potential plagiarism accusation, a whisper of an investigation into her recent submissions. It was all manufactured, of course, but the manual had taught him how effective the *implication* of such things could be. A few carefully worded, anonymous emails, hinting at a review of her academic record, coupled with the 'accidental' discovery of a similar research paper on a public database—a paper that, while superficially similar, was demonstrably different upon closer inspection—was enough to sow the seeds of panic. He had seen her flinch when a professor called her name, seen her shoulders tense when she overheard hushed conversations in the hallway. She was a bright spark, and he was systematically dampening her flame, enjoying the dimming of her ambition, the creeping fear that she might be on the verge of a catastrophic professional downfall.

And Mr. Peterson, the fastidious librarian, whose world of order he had so artfully disrupted. Adam hadn't directly interacted with him again, but he had observed from a distance. Peterson's meticulously organized desk was no longer a testament to his precision, but to his increasing frailty. Papers were slightly askew, pens were not perfectly aligned, and a faint air of disarray had begun to permeate his usually immaculate workspace. Adam suspected his earlier subtle interventions—the slight repositioning of frequently used items, the almost imperceptible alteration of cataloging systems—had chipped away at Peterson's unwavering sense of control. The manual had a section on 'exploiting obsessions,' and Peterson's obsession with order was a glaring vulnerability. Adam had introduced just enough chaos to make Peterson question his own sanity, to wonder if he was losing his touch, if the meticulously crafted order of his world was finally succumbing to an unseen entropy. The thought of Peterson's quiet frustration, his silent struggle to maintain his perfect equilibrium, was a subtle, yet persistent, source of amusement for Adam.

These were no longer mere exercises. The detached fascination had curdled into something else, something hungrier. The manual was no longer a guide; it was a blueprint, and Adam was the eager architect of its terrifying designs. He found himself sketching out scenarios in his mind, elaborating on the initial manipulations, pushing the boundaries of what he had previously considered possible. His satisfaction was no longer a fleeting intellectual triumph, but a deep, resonant hum that pulsed through his very being. He was becoming addicted to the feeling of power, the visceral thrill of watching minds unravel under his subtle, yet relentless, pressure. The library, once a haven of quiet contemplation, had transformed into his private laboratory, a stage upon which he conducted his increasingly elaborate psychological experiments. Each twitch of fear, each flicker of doubt, was a testament to his growing mastery.

He began to look for new challenges, new subjects to test his evolving skills upon. He found himself observing the library patrons with a predatory gaze, sifting through their routines, their habits, their subtle tells, searching for the cracks in their carefully constructed exteriors. He saw not people, but potential subjects, their vulnerabilities laid bare for his discerning eye. The manual's chapters on 'cultivating paranoia,' 'inducing social isolation,' and even 'triggering latent trauma' began to seem less like theoretical concepts and more like practical guides for his next performance.

There was the young student, always hunched over his laptop, a solitary figure lost in the digital world. Adam had noticed a subtle nervous habit – a constant flicking of his gaze towards the library's main entrance. The manual's section on 'environmental manipulation' came to mind. Adam began to orchestrate small, almost imperceptible events. A sudden, unexplained draft that would sweep through the area, rustling papers and causing the student to jump. The intermittent flickering of the lights, just enough to be noticeable and unnerving. The occasional, distant thud from somewhere within the library's cavernous structure, sounds that could easily be dismissed by a casual observer, but which, to someone already on edge, could signify something more sinister. He even found himself subtly altering the library's background hum, introducing a barely audible, high-frequency tone that he knew could induce a sense of unease and agitation. He watched as the student's nervous habit intensified, his visits becoming shorter, his focus increasingly fractured. He was building a cage of perceived threats, brick by invisible brick.

Then there was the elderly woman who always sat by the window, knitting with delicate precision. Her face was a picture of serene contentment, but Adam sensed a fragility beneath the surface. He recalled a passage in the manual about 'leveraging past regrets.' He began to leave carefully selected 'lost' items near her table - a faded photograph, a child's worn toy, a forgotten letter. He would then discreetly observe her reactions, noting any flicker of recognition, any subtle shift in her demeanor. He even commissioned a local artist, under the guise of a personal project, to create a series of seemingly innocuous sketches of the library, subtly incorporating elements that might trigger a specific, buried memory. He was playing a long game, not just with her present, but with her past, intending to excavate and amplify any lingering sorrow or regret. The thought of her quiet tears, shed over a manufactured ghost of her own history, was a darkly appealing prospect.

His 'games' were evolving, becoming more complex, more intertwined. He no longer felt the need for overt confrontation. The subtle nudges, the whispered suggestions, the carefully curated environments were proving far more effective, and infinitely more satisfying. He was a conductor of discord, his orchestra comprised of the unsuspecting souls who graced the hallowed halls of the library. The manual, his sacred text, seemed to pulse with a life of its own, its ink glowing with the dark magic he was so eagerly embracing. The satisfaction he derived was no longer solely intellectual; it was a visceral, almost physical sensation, a current of raw power that coursed through him with every successful manipulation. He reveled in the increasing vulnerability of his subjects, their carefully constructed realities beginning to crumble under the weight of his unseen influence.

But with this growing power came a darker awareness. He began to notice the subtle shifts within himself. The initial curiosity, the intellectual pursuit of understanding human behavior, had transformed into a hunger, a craving for the very unraveling he was orchestrating. The thrill was no longer just in the execution of the plan, but in the sheer spectacle of the collapse. He found himself lingering after his 'interventions,' observing the aftermath with a detached intensity, cataloging the subtle signs of distress, the bewildered expressions, the heightened anxieties. He was no longer just an observer; he was a predator, and the library was his hunting ground.

The manual's later chapters, previously skimmed over as theoretical or extreme, now held a morbid fascination. He found himself rereading passages on 'escalation tactics,' on 'creating irreversible damage,' and the words seemed to resonate with a chilling new understanding. The innocent experiments with anxiety and doubt felt like a distant memory, a pale prelude to the darker possibilities that now beckoned. He saw the potential for destruction, for true, lasting harm, and a part of him, a deeply buried, newly awakened part, craved it.

He started to see the world differently. People were no longer complex individuals with their own unique struggles and joys. They were patterns of behavior, predictable responses to stimuli, vulnerabilities waiting to be exploited. His social interactions, once a chore, became opportunities to hone his craft, to practice his subtle art of manipulation. He found it increasingly difficult to engage in genuine connection, his mind constantly analyzing, dissecting, searching for an angle, a weakness. The warmth of human interaction felt alien, replaced by the cold, calculated precision of his chosen path.

One evening, as he walked home, the city lights blurring into streaks of color, he caught his reflection in a darkened shop window. For a fleeting moment, he didn't recognize the face staring back at him. The eyes, once filled with a quiet curiosity, now held a glint of something sharp and predatory. A shadow seemed to have lengthened behind him, stretching and distorting his reflection, hinting at a darkness that had taken root within his soul. He knew, with a chilling certainty, that he was no longer the same person who had first picked up the manual. The allure of the unseen had become an obsession, a consuming fire that was reshaping him into something entirely new, something far more terrifying than he could have ever imagined. The library was no longer just a place; it was the crucible in which Adam Tapper was forging his new, terrifying persona, and the world outside its walls was about to bear witness to the darkness he had so carefully cultivated. The next chapter, he knew, would not be about subtle nudges or manufactured anxieties. It would be about the true consequences of his actions, the unfolding horrors that lay just beyond the horizon, and he, Adam Tapper, would be the architect of it all.

Chapter 2: The Weight of Justice Denied

The scent of stale coffee and photocopier toner was Gwen Staples's constant companion. It clung to her uniform, permeated her tiny office, and seemed to seep into her very pores. Detective Staples, a name whispered with a mixture of grudging respect and exasperated sigh throughout the precinct, was known for her unwavering tenacity. She possessed a sharp, analytical mind, a healthy distrust of easy answers, and a moral compass that stubbornly pointed true north, even when the prevailing winds of departmental politics threatened to blow it askew. Her colleagues often joked that she had a personal vendetta against unresolved cases, that she treated every cold file as a personal affront. The truth was, Gwen didn't just see cases; she saw the shattered lives left in their wake, the gaping holes in families, the silent pleas for justice that echoed in the empty spaces.

Her current caseload was a testament to her reputation – a steady stream of the city's uglier truths, each one demanding her full attention. But beneath the professional veneer, a deeper, more personal wound festered, a ghost that haunted her waking hours and stalked her dreams. It was the case that had nearly broken her, the one she carried like a shard of glass embedded in her heart: the murder of her younger brother, Michael.

It had been three years now, three years of the gnawing emptiness where his laughter used to be, three years of replaying their last conversation, searching for a clue, a warning sign she might have missed. Michael, always the artist, the dreamer, had somehow found himself entangled in something dangerous, something far removed from the vibrant canvases he once painted. Gwen had been the one to discover his body, a scene so brutal, so senseless, that it had seared itself into her memory, a permanent stain on her psyche.

From that moment on, the investigation had consumed her. She had thrown herself into it with a ferocity that bordered on obsession, fueled by a potent cocktail of grief, rage, and a burning desire for retribution. She had followed every lead, interviewed every potential witness, pieced together fragments of Michael's final days with a meticulousness that impressed even her jaded superiors. She had identified a prime suspect, a local loan shark with a reputation for violence, and had amassed a mountain of circumstantial evidence. The pieces were falling into place, the narrative of Michael's demise becoming sickeningly clear. She could almost taste the impending arrest, the sweet relief of seeing justice served, of finally being able to close the book on this agonizing chapter.

She remembered the night vividly. The air in her cramped office was thick with tension, the only illumination cast by the harsh glare of her desk lamp. Maps littered the surface, crisscrossed with red marker lines, connecting a web of shady characters and illicit dealings. Photographs of Michael, vibrant and full of life, were tacked to the corkboard, a stark contrast to the grainy surveillance stills of her suspect. She had spent hours poring over financial records, tracking drug deals, and cross-referencing alibis, her eyes burning, her mind a hyper-focused machine. She felt a surge of adrenaline, the exhilarating certainty of being on the precipice of a breakthrough.

She had compiled a detailed report, outlining her findings and presenting a compelling case for an immediate warrant. She had presented it to her immediate superior, Captain Davies, a man who had always shown her a paternal sort of respect. He had read it slowly, his brow furrowed in concentration, and when he finally looked up, there was a flicker of something unreadable in his eyes – not doubt, but something akin to resignation.

“Staples,” he had said, his voice low, “This is… thorough. Damned thorough. You’ve done good work. Real good work.”

Gwen had allowed herself a small, triumphant smile. “Thank you, Captain. I think we have enough.”

Davies had sighed, a heavy, weary sound. He had reached for a file on his own desk, a thin, nondescript folder. “That’s where it gets complicated, Gwen.”

He slid the file across the desk. Her name wasn’t on it, nor Michael’s. It was a case she vaguely recalled being flagged for internal affairs, a messy business involving high-profile individuals and allegations of corruption.

“Chief Vance wants you off this, Gwen,” Davies had said, his gaze direct but compassionate. “He wants you to hand over everything you’ve got on Michael’s case to Detective Miller, and focus on this new assignment.”

The blood had drained from Gwen’s face. “Chief Vance? But… why? This is Michael’s case. I’m this close to closing it.” She gestured wildly at the papers spread before her, her voice rising with disbelief and dawning horror. “That loan shark, Marco Bellucci… he’s our guy. I have the evidence.”

“I know,” Davies had replied, his tone apologetic. “And you’ve done an exceptional job. But Vance… he’s got his reasons. Politics, Gwen. You know how it is. This other case… it’s got some very powerful people involved. People the Chief can’t afford to alienate.

He sees you as… expendable on this one. A loose end he needs to tie up, or rather, a loose end he needs to redirect before it causes him trouble."

Gwen had stared at him, her mind struggling to process his words. Expendable? Michael's murder, her brother's life, reduced to a political inconvenience? The anger, a slow burn until now, erupted into a searing inferno. "He can't do this! This is my brother! He *ordered* me to stay off it before, when I first started sniffing around Bellucci. He said it was a 'sensitive matter.' Sensitive? Is that what he calls murder now? A 'sensitive matter' that doesn't fit his dirty little agenda?"

"Gwen, I understand you're upset," Davies had said, his voice laced with genuine sympathy. "But you have two choices. You can refuse, and risk an official reprimand, potentially losing your badge. Or you can do as you're told, and maybe, just maybe, find a way to revisit this down the line, from a different angle."

The injustice of it all had choked her. The sheer, suffocating weight of the system, designed to protect and serve, instead seemed intent on crushing the very people it was meant to uphold. Chief Vance, a man she had once admired for his no-nonsense approach, now appeared as a cynical architect of compromise, sacrificing truth on the altar of political expediency. And Marco Bellucci, the man responsible for her brother's death, would walk free, his reign of terror unopposed, all because of a few phone calls from people in high places.

She had walked out of Davies's office that night feeling a cold, hard knot of resentment settle deep within her. She had been forced to hand over her meticulously gathered evidence, her hard-won progress, to Detective Miller, a competent but uninspired officer who lacked her personal investment. She had watched as the investigation into Michael's murder lost its momentum, the urgency replaced by a bureaucratic shuffle. Bellucci, as expected, remained untouched, his smirking face a constant torment in her thoughts.

The assignment Vance had thrust upon her was indeed a political minefield, a tangled web of influence peddling and questionable financial dealings that threatened to ensnare several prominent city officials. It was a case designed to keep a sharp detective busy, to distract them from more pressing matters – or, in Gwen's case, to simply keep her out of the way. She approached it with a grim determination, her mind a battlefield where her professional duty warred with her personal anguish. Every dead end, every bureaucratic hurdle, every veiled threat from the higher-ups only fueled the simmering anger that lay beneath her calm exterior. She learned to navigate the treacherous currents of departmental politics, to play the game without compromising her integrity, all the while nurturing a deep-seated loathing for the man who had stolen her brother's justice and, in doing so, had irrevocably altered her own. The badge she wore, once a symbol of pride and purpose, now felt like a brand, a constant reminder of the justice denied, the case that would forever haunt her. This was not just a job anymore; it was a long, drawn-out war, fought in the shadows of the law, with the ghost of her brother Michael as her silent, unwavering ally.

The sterile, acrid scent of the Chief's office was a stark contrast to the familiar, comforting musk of Gwen's own workspace. Here, the air hummed with a different kind of tension, a hushed formality that spoke of power and consequence. Chief Vance sat behind a desk that was impossibly large, impossibly clean, a polished obsidian monolith that seemed to swallow any light that dared to enter the room. His face, usually a mask of impassive authority, was etched with a weariness that Gwen recognized – the same weariness she saw in Captain Davies's eyes, but amplified, hardened by years of navigating the treacherous currents of city politics.

"Detective Staples," Vance began, his voice a low rumble, devoid of the warmth or even the gruff camaraderie that sometimes surfaced in the precinct hallways. He didn't offer a handshake, nor did he meet her gaze directly, his eyes fixed on a point somewhere beyond her left shoulder. "Captain Davies informs me you've compiled a rather... comprehensive report on the Michael Staples case."

The use of her brother's full name, spoken with such clinical detachment, sent a fresh wave of ice through Gwen's veins. She tightened her grip on the worn leather portfolio clutched in her hands. "Yes, Chief. I believe I have enough to secure a warrant for Marco Bellucci."

Vance finally looked at her, and the expression in his eyes was not one of admiration for her work, but a subtle, chilling assessment. It was the look of a man weighing assets and liabilities, a predator calculating the cost of a kill. "Bellucci," he mused, the name rolling off his tongue with an almost imperceptible disdain. "A common thug. Easily dealt with, one would think."

"He murdered my brother, Chief," Gwen stated, her voice deliberately even, betraying none of the tremor that threatened to shake her to her core. "And he's responsible for numerous other violent crimes. The evidence is clear."

A dismissive flick of Vance's wrist. "Evidence is a funny thing, Detective. It can be interpreted. Twisted. Sometimes, the simplest explanation isn't the most... politically expedient." He leaned back in his chair, the leather groaning softly beneath his weight. “You’ve been working this case with a… singular focus, Gwen. admirable, in its way. But you’ve also become rather… emotionally invested.”

The implication hung heavy in the air. Emotionally invested. As if her grief and her righteous fury were a professional failing, a contamination of her objectivity. “My brother was murdered, Chief. I’m not asking for vengeance, I’m asking for justice. The kind of justice this badge is supposed to represent.”

Vance chuckled, a dry, rasping sound that was more unsettling than outright anger. “Justice, Staples, is a luxury. And sometimes, it’s a luxury the city can’t afford. Not when it involves certain… complications.” He tapped his polished desk with a manicured finger. “Bellucci might be a thug, but he’s a small-time thug. The kind of fish that swims in shallow waters. The kind that doesn’t attract much attention when it washes ashore.”

He paused, letting the unspoken words settle between them. Gwen felt a prickle of unease crawling up her spine. This wasn’t just about politics; there was something deeper, something Vance was carefully obscuring.

“However,” he continued, his tone shifting, taking on a more official, directive quality. “There have been a series of recent homicides. Unrelated, on the surface. A convenience store clerk in the East End, a dockworker down by the river, a young woman found in an alleyway in the Financial District. All brutal, all with little to no immediate leads. These cases are… sensitive. They’re generating heat. The press is sniffing around. The Mayor’s office is getting antsy. And frankly, Detective, your… intensity on the Staples case, while commendable, has made you a distraction.”

Gwen’s breath hitched. A distraction. Michael’s murder, her brother’s life, reduced to an inconvenient roadblock in Vance’s meticulously constructed political landscape. “A distraction from what, Chief? From letting a killer walk free?”

Vance’s gaze hardened. “A distraction from the needs of the department, Staples. From the cases that have the potential to destabilize the city, to erode public trust. These new homicides require a sharp mind, a detached perspective. Someone who can see the forest for the trees. And right now, you’re too consumed by your own personal woods.”

He gestured towards a thick manila folder lying innocuously on the corner of his desk. Gwen’s blood ran cold as she recognized the faded departmental seal. “This is your new assignment. Detective Harding will be taking over the primary investigation into your brother's murder. He'll be briefed by Captain Davies. I expect you to cooperate fully, to hand over all your findings. And I expect you to dedicate yourself to these new cases. No more digging into Bellucci. No more... personal crusades. This is an order, Detective."

The weight of his words pressed down on her, a physical force threatening to buckle her knees. Harding. A competent man, yes, but one who lacked her understanding of the city's underbelly, her gut instinct, her intimate knowledge of the players involved. He would be a puppet, dancing to the tune of whoever truly pulled the strings. And she, the one who had bled and sweat and grieved over Michael's case, was being sidelined, relegated to a series of seemingly random, unconnected tragedies.

"Chief," Gwen said, her voice barely a whisper, her carefully constructed composure threatening to shatter. "You're asking me to let him go. You're asking me to turn my back on my brother."

Vance's expression remained impassive, a granite facade that offered no room for empathy. "I'm asking you to do your job, Detective. As you are ordered. These new cases are high priority. Failure to address them effectively will have consequences. Not just for you, but for the department. And for the city." He leaned forward, his voice dropping to a near-whisper, a silken threat laced with the promise of power. "I value your skills, Staples. I wouldn't have kept you on the force if I didn't. But I also expect loyalty. And obedience. You can either be a valuable asset, or a persistent problem. The choice, ultimately, is yours."

The unspoken threat resonated in the silence that followed. Resist, and risk everything. Cooperate, and betray her brother's memory. The confrontation was over, but the battle had just begun. As Gwen rose, her legs feeling heavy, alien, she knew she was walking out of Vance's office not just with a new assignment, but with a heavy, suffocating burden. The weight of justice denied, amplified by the very institution sworn to uphold it. The path ahead was shrouded in shadow, and the whispers of political expediency seemed to drown out the silent plea for truth.

The city, usually a symphony of blaring sirens and restless nightlife, had begun to hum with a discordant new tune. A low thrum of unease, growing louder with each passing day, each grim headline. The air, once thick with the scent of exhaust fumes and street food, now carried a subtle, almost imperceptible undercurrent of fear. It clung to the brickwork of the older neighborhoods, seeped into the gleaming chrome of the business district, and whispered through the leafy avenues of the suburbs. This wasn't the usual urban anxiety, the fleeting jitters of a city that never truly slept. This was a gnawing apprehension, a collective holding of breath as the shadows lengthened and the news of another life extinguished began to spread like a contagion.

Gwen felt it the moment she stepped out of Vance's suffocatingly controlled office, a palpable shift in the city's energy that mirrored the chilling directives she had just received. The precinct itself, usually a chaotic hive of activity, seemed to have been inoculated with the same somber mood. Officers moved with a weary efficiency, their faces etched with a fatigue that went beyond the usual grind of long hours. Conversations were hushed, punctuated by furtive glances and the rustle of case files. The casual banter, the rough camaraderie that usually permeated the squad room, had evaporated, replaced by a grim solidarity in the face of an encroaching darkness.

The first of the new reports had landed on Captain Davies's desk with a quiet thud, a stark contrast to the clamor that had surrounded Michael's case. Now, it felt as though the floodgates had opened. The East End convenience store, a brightly lit beacon of late-night convenience, had become a crime scene. The clerk, a man Gwen vaguely recognized from her patrols, a quiet immigrant who worked tirelessly to support his family, had been found behind the counter, his life brutally and senselessly ended. The details, leaked through the precinct's grapevine, were sparse but chilling: a single, precise wound, no signs of forced entry, no robbery. Just a void where a life had been.

Then came the dockworker, a burly, salt-of-the-earth type whose usual shift ended with the clatter of crates and the roar of forklifts. He'd been discovered near the river's edge, the muddy banks swallowing any trace of the struggle, the official report citing blunt force trauma, a methodical, almost clinical execution. The press, ever hungry for sensationalism, latched onto the growing number of fatalities, weaving a narrative of a city under siege, a creeping menace that targeted the unsuspecting, the ordinary.

And just days later, the young woman. Found in an alleyway in the heart of the Financial District, a place usually pulsating with ambition and wealth, now stained by an act of unimaginable violence. Her story, as it emerged, was a poignant counterpoint to the grim reality of her demise. A recent graduate, full of promise, just starting her career, her life cut short before it had truly begun. The brutality of her death, the sheer lack of any apparent motive, sent a fresh wave of revulsion through the city.

Each victim, a distinct thread in the tapestry of urban life, yet their endings were eerily similar. Varied backgrounds, disparate lives, but a shared, chillingly efficient demise. There was no obvious pattern, no discernible link between a shopkeeper in the East End, a laborer by the river, and a young professional in the financial hub. They were random, terrifyingly so. The precision of the killings, the absence of struggle or excess violence beyond what was necessary to achieve the fatal outcome, spoke of a chilling professionalism, a cold, calculated intent that sent shivers down Gwen's spine. It was the signature of a predator, not a common thug fueled by rage or desperation.

The public, bombarded by fragmented reports and the constant hum of media speculation, began to retreat behind locked doors. The vibrant street life, the spontaneous gatherings, the easy camaraderie between strangers – all began to recede, replaced by a palpable sense of vulnerability. Parents clutched their children tighter, late-night workers hurried their steps, and the city's rhythm faltered, its usual confidence replaced by a growing, collective anxiety. The mayor's office, Vance had said, was getting antsy. That was an understatement. The city council was abuzz with urgent meetings, and the phones in the precinct were ringing off the hook with calls from concerned citizens, frantic pleas for reassurance that the police were in control, that this wave of terror would be stemmed.

The strain on the police department was immense. Detectives, already stretched thin by the relentless demands of their city, were now facing an onslaught of cases that were as baffling as they were brutal. Resources were being diverted, priorities shifted, and the whisper of "high priority" began to echo through the halls, a constant reminder of the immense pressure from above. Gwen, her own grief a raw, open wound, was now tasked with navigating this escalating crisis, a crisis that demanded her full attention, her unwavering focus, at a time when her own world had been irrevocably fractured. The weight of her brother's case, once a driving force, now felt like a leaden anchor, threatening to drag her down as she was forced to swim in these dark, turbulent waters. She saw the exhaustion in the eyes of her colleagues, the quiet desperation of those trying to piece together fragmented clues, and she knew this was just the beginning. The city was under siege, not by an invading army, but by a faceless enemy who moved in the shadows, leaving behind only terror and an ever-growing sense of dread. The initial reports painted a grim picture, a mosaic of fear and unanswered questions, and Gwen knew, with a sickening certainty, that she was now a reluctant participant in a much larger, much darker narrative. The sheer diversity of the victims was, in itself, a horrifying indicator of the killer's reach, or perhaps, a deliberate attempt to sow maximum discord and panic. A homeless man found in the park a few nights later, a respected judge discovered in his study, a teenage runaway with no prior record – the list grew, each new victim a fresh stab of fear into the heart of the city. The press, initially focusing on the individual tragedies, began to draw parallels, albeit tenuous ones, between the disparate victims. A hushed whisper of a serial killer began to circulate, a phantom moving through the city's arteries, leaving death in his wake.

The brutality was consistent, a hallmark of the killer's grim artistry. Not just murder, but a statement. Sometimes it was overkill, a savage frenzy that seemed to contradict the otherwise precise nature of the fatal wound. Other times, it was starkly minimal, as if the act itself was the sole objective, devoid of any emotional outburst. This inconsistency, this lack of a clear, singular modus operandi, was what truly unnerved the seasoned investigators. It made profiling a nightmare, any attempt to categorize the killer falling apart under the weight of contradictory evidence. It was as if the killer was toying with them, deliberately blurring the lines, ensuring that no single theory could take root.

The police department, usually a bastion of order in the urban chaos, found itself struggling to maintain its footing. Patrol officers, accustomed to responding to petty crimes and domestic disputes, were now on high alert, their radios crackling with reports of suspicious activity in every corner of the city. Detectives, accustomed to the methodical pursuit of leads, found themselves chasing ghosts, their investigations often hitting dead ends before they had even truly begun. The sheer volume of cases was overwhelming, each one demanding immediate attention, each one a potential key to unlocking the horrifying truth. Overtime became the norm, sleep a luxury, and the precinct cafeteria, once a hub of weary but convivial camaraderie, transformed into a silent testament to exhaustion, its occupants hunched over lukewarm coffee and cold sandwiches, their faces gaunt, their eyes hollow.

The fear, however, was not confined to the ranks of law enforcement. It had permeated the city's consciousness. Every creak of a floorboard, every shadow that danced at the edge of vision, became a potential threat. The vibrant street art that usually adorned the city's underpasses and alleyways seemed to mock the newfound fear, its colorful expressions of life now juxtaposed against the grim reality of death. Graffiti that once proclaimed unity and rebellion now bore slogans of caution and despair. People began to walk with their heads down, their senses on high alert, their eyes scanning not for friends or familiar faces, but for anything that seemed out of place, anything that could signal danger. The city, once a vibrant, pulsating entity, was slowly, inexorably, succumbing to a collective paranoia. The sense of security, the implicit trust that the city's protectors would keep them safe, was eroding with each passing day. This wasn't just about a few isolated incidents; it was a creeping, insidious terror that threatened to unravel the very fabric of the community. The pressure on Vance, and by extension, on Gwen, was immense. The whispers from the Mayor's office were no longer whispers; they were demands, urgent and insistent, for results, for a swift resolution to the growing crisis. And Gwen, burdened by the weight of her brother's unsolved murder and the daunting prospect of these new, interconnected tragedies, could feel the city's fear pressing in on her, a suffocating shroud that threatened to extinguish even the smallest flicker of hope. The very streets she had once patrolled with a sense of purpose now felt alien and hostile, each corner a potential ambush, each passerby a possible threat. This was the grim backdrop against which her own personal crusade was now forced to play out, a chilling prelude to a darkness she was only beginning to comprehend.

The air in Gwen's cramped office was thick with the stale scent of old coffee and printer toner, a familiar perfume of late nights and unsolved cases. She'd retreated here, seeking refuge from the suffocating hum of the precinct floor, the unspoken anxieties that hung heavy in the air like a pre-storm humidity. The initial reports were spread across her desk, a stark visual representation of the city's unraveling – the convenience store clerk, the dockworker, the young professional, each a tragedy in its own right. Individually, they were brutal, senseless acts that fueled the public's growing fear. But Gwen had a gut feeling, a prickling sensation that refused to be dismissed. She'd seen enough to know that sometimes, the most chilling truths lay hidden beneath the surface, disguised in plain sight.

She ran a weary hand over her eyes, the fluorescent lights overhead casting harsh shadows that deepened the lines of fatigue around them. Captain Davies had been clear: focus on the current surge, put Michael's case on the back burner. But how could she? Every new victim, every chilling detail, felt like a phantom limb, a painful echo of her brother's own brutal end. She'd been tasked with wading through the mounting evidence, sifting through the debris of these new lives extinguished, and the more she looked, the more the disparate threads began to weave a disturbing tapestry.

The convenience store. Ramiro Diaz. A man who'd greeted her with a shy smile and a nod every time she'd stopped for a late-night snack. No forced entry. The cash register untouched. The murder weapon, a single, clean stab wound, precise and almost surgical. The paramedics had noted it in their preliminary report: a remarkable lack of disarray, no sign of a struggle beyond what was necessary to inflict the fatal injury. It was as if Ramiro had simply… collapsed. A chilling efficiency that didn't fit the profile of a panicked robber.

Then there was Frank Kowalski, the dockworker. Found near Pier 17, his heavy work boots caked in mud. The autopsy report described blunt force trauma, multiple blows, but delivered with a strange, almost restrained force. Not the frenzied rage of a bar fight gone wrong, nor the desperate, wild swings of a mugger. The report mentioned a specific point of impact, a concentration of force that suggested a targeted strike rather than a random assault. And his wallet was still in his pocket, a significant amount of cash still tucked inside. Another anomaly.

And Sarah Jenkins, the bright young analyst found in that back alley behind the gleaming towers of the Financial District. Her expensive handbag lay beside her, its contents spilled onto the grimy pavement – a scattered collection of lipstick, a crumpled metro card, a small notebook. Nothing appeared to be missing. The cause of death, again, a single, precise wound. No defensive wounds. No signs of sexual assault. The forensic team noted the meticulous nature of the scene, an almost surgical cleanliness that belied the barbarity of the act. It was as if the killer had taken great care to ensure that nothing was out of place, as if the crime itself was an exhibition, its details carefully curated.

Gwen leaned back in her chair, the worn springs groaning in protest. These weren't random acts. Not entirely. The lack of robbery, the almost clinical precision of the fatal wounds, the absence of significant struggle – these were not the hallmarks of opportunistic violence. They spoke of something else. Something planned. Something... deliberate. She felt a familiar chill creep up her spine, a sensation that had become all too familiar in the wake of Michael's death. This felt disturbingly familiar, like echoes of darker, more complex schemes.

She pulled out the file on Michael's case, the thin Manila folder a stark contrast to the thicker stacks of the new reports. The details were etched into her memory, a scar she carried daily. The single gunshot wound, perfectly placed. The lack of a clear motive. The baffling lack of any concrete leads. Vance had dismissed it as a street crime gone wrong, a random act of violence in a city that had too much of it. But Gwen had never accepted that. She'd seen the careful staging of the scene, the way the weapon had been placed, the unnerving tidiness of the aftermath. It had felt too deliberate, too... rehearsed.

Now, looking at Ramiro's, Frank's, and Sarah's files, the similarities were becoming too stark to ignore. A pattern, however subtle, was beginning to emerge. It wasn't the typical serial killer signature – no specific victimology, no consistent method of murder beyond the precision of the fatal blow. But there was a quiet, almost artistic tidiness to each scene. An absence of the usual chaos that accompanied such violent encounters. It was as if the perpetrator was not just killing, but meticulously orchestrating each event, ensuring that the aftermath was as clean as the act itself.

Gwen's fingers traced the lines of the autopsy report for Ramiro Diaz. "Single stab wound to the thoracic cavity, entering between the third and fourth intercostal spaces, penetrating the pericardium and causing immediate cardiac arrest." The language was cold, clinical, but the implications sent a shiver down her spine. This wasn't a wild, frenzied stabbing. This was precise. Measured. It required a level of knowledge, a steady hand, and a terrifying calmness.

She then turned to Frank Kowalski's file. Blunt force trauma. But the report highlighted a specific area of impact on the skull, a fracture that indicated a concentrated blow. Not a barrage of random hits. One, perhaps two, well-aimed strikes. The coroner had even commented on the efficiency of the assault, noting that it would have rendered the victim incapacitated almost instantly. Again, the absence of a significant struggle. Frank was a big man, strong. He wouldn't have gone down easily without putting up a fight. Yet, the scene suggested otherwise.

And Sarah Jenkins. The same sterile precision. The same lack of extraneous violence. It was as if the killer was a sculptor, chipping away at the excess, leaving only the essential act of death.

What was the common thread? A shopkeeper, a laborer, a financial analyst. No shared social circles, no obvious connections. Their ages, their backgrounds, their routines were all vastly different. It defied easy categorization. But the *method*, the almost surgical execution, the unnerving *order* in the chaos – that was the anomaly. It spoke of a mind that was not driven by primal rage or impulsive lust. It spoke of calculation. Control.

Gwen's gaze drifted back to Michael's file. His death had been a clean shot. One bullet. No wasted movement. And the scene had been eerily undisturbed. Vance had chalked it up to a professional hit, a hired gun. But now, with these new cases, a different, more insidious possibility began to form. What if it wasn't a hired gun, but a single individual, meticulously carrying out a series of acts that, while varied in their specifics, shared a common, chilling design?

She remembered the whispers in the precinct after Michael's death, the hushed theories about a lone wolf, a phantom killer who moved in and out of the city's underbelly, leaving no trace. At the time, it had seemed too fantastical, too much like something out of a cheap paperback. But now...

The press was having a field day, of course. Headlines screamed about a city gripped by fear, a predator on the loose. They were focusing on the sheer number of victims, the diverse backgrounds, the growing sense of vulnerability. But they were missing the subtle details, the almost imperceptible anomalies that were screaming at Gwen from the pages of these reports. They were seeing the forest, but Gwen was starting to see the individual, meticulously placed trees.

She picked up a coffee mug, its ceramic cool against her fingertips. Was it possible that these were not separate incidents at all, but part of a larger, more intricate plan? A plan designed to sow fear, to destabilize, to... what? The motive remained elusive, a ghost in the machine. But the *intelligence* behind it, the sheer calculated precision, was undeniable. It felt less like a spree and more like a campaign.

Gwen began to pull out the crime scene photos, laying them out on the desk. The stark, sterile lighting of the morgue contrasted with the grimy realism of the alleyways and the quiet normalcy of the convenience store. She stared at the images, trying to see beyond the gore, beyond the tragedy, to the underlying structure. The placement of the bodies, the way the minimal evidence had been collected, the initial witness statements – she reviewed them all with a renewed intensity.

The convenience store's security footage had been... unhelpful. A grainy black-and-white recording that showed Ramiro locking up, then a flicker of movement, a shadow, and then nothing until the first responding officers arrived. The killer had been a phantom, a glitch in the system. The same with Frank Kowalski. No witnesses. Just the lingering scent of diesel and the distant cry of seagulls. Sarah Jenkins's attack had been in a blind spot, a gap in the otherwise ubiquitous surveillance network of the Financial District. It was as if the killer knew where to strike, where to avoid detection.

This wasn't just about violence; it was about strategy. It was about precision. It was about leaving the least amount of trace possible. Gwen felt a knot tighten in her stomach. This wasn't the work of a common criminal. This was something far more complex. Something that felt disturbingly familiar, like a melody she'd heard before but couldn't quite place. A melody played in a minor key, laced with a chilling dissonance.

She remembered Michael's obsession with unsolved cases, his late-night dives into criminal psychology, his fascination with patterns. He'd often talked about how killers, even the most deranged, often had an internal logic, a set of rules they followed, even if those rules were twisted. He'd said that the more you understood the logic, the closer you got to understanding the killer.

And Gwen was beginning to see the logic here, the almost mathematical elegance of the violence. The efficiency of the kills, the lack of unnecessary mess, the strategic avoidance of detection. It was all part of a deliberate design. But what was the ultimate purpose?

She closed her eyes, picturing Michael's face, his earnest gaze when he'd explain some obscure criminological theory. "*It's not about the 'why' at first, Gwen,*" he'd said, his voice animated. "*It's about the 'how.' The how tells you about the who. The how tells you about the intent. The 'why' comes later.*"

The how. The how was the precision. The how was the tidiness. The how was the almost surgical removal of life. And the how was starting to whisper a name, a possibility that Gwen had been too afraid to even consider. A possibility that connected Michael's death to these new horrors, not as a random act, but as a prelude.

She opened her eyes, her gaze falling on a small, almost insignificant detail in Ramiro Diaz's file. A single, stray fiber found near the body, not matching anything in the victim's clothing or the store's inventory. It had been logged, cataloged, and likely filed away as an anomaly, a piece of forensic detritus. But Gwen stared at it, a flicker of recognition igniting in her mind. It was a distinctive weave, a specific color. Where had she seen it before?

Her heart began to pound against her ribs, a frantic drumbeat against the quiet of her office. She fumbled through Michael's case file, her fingers shaking slightly as she searched for any similar anomalies, any overlooked details that might have been dismissed as irrelevant. And then she found it. A similar fiber. Found near the scene of Michael's shooting. It had been logged as an unknown, an insignificant piece of lint. But it wasn't lint. It was the same weave, the same color.

The carefully constructed walls of Gwen's composure began to crumble. It wasn't a coincidence. It couldn't be. The precision. The tidiness. The same anomalous fiber. The echoes were too strong, the connections too undeniable. These weren't random acts. This was something far more calculated, far more sinister. And it was deeply, terrifyingly familiar. The weight of justice denied, for Michael and for these new victims, settled upon her shoulders, heavier than ever before. The city's fear was palpable, but Gwen's was a cold, sharp dread, a premonition of a darkness that was far more organized, and far more dangerous, than anyone had yet dared to imagine. The pattern wasn't just emerging; it was staring her in the face, a chilling testament to a mind that was as brilliant as it was brutal.

The subtle threads of connection, initially faint and easily dismissed as the product of a grief-addled mind, were now weaving themselves into a tapestry of undeniable horror. Gwen stared at the fibers, the minuscule strands of evidence that had been deemed insignificant by others, but which now pulsed with a sinister significance in her mind. Ramiro's file lay open, the sterile white of the lab report a stark contrast to the dark implications of its findings. The fiber, a deep, almost bruised shade of indigo, was described as a "synthetic blend, likely from high-performance apparel." It was a detail so small, so easily overlooked, yet it was the very element that made Gwen's blood run cold. She remembered the specific texture of the fabric, the way it had snagged on the rough concrete near where Michael's body had been found. A detail she had almost forgotten, buried beneath the crushing weight of her initial shock and despair.

The precinct hummed with a low-grade anxiety, a collective unease that permeated the very air. The news channels blared sensational headlines, painting a picture of a city teetering on the brink of chaos. But while the public and the media fixated on the rising body count and the random nature of the victims, Gwen was drawn to the meticulous artistry of the crimes. The chilling tidiness that accompanied each violent act was not just a signature; it was a statement. It spoke of a mind that was not only capable of great violence but also possessed an unnerving level of control and a profound understanding of... something. A system? A methodology? She couldn't quite articulate it, but the feeling persisted – a sense of calculated precision that transcended mere criminality.

She sifted through Sarah Jenkins's file again, her gaze lingering on the crime scene photographs. The young woman lay on the grimy pavement, her life extinguished with an almost surgical finality. The absence of a struggle was palpable, even in the static images. No torn clothing, no defensive wounds, no overturned debris that might indicate a desperate fight for survival. It was as if Sarah had simply... ceased to exist. The meticulous arrangement of her belongings, the spilled contents of her handbag laid out like an exhibit, felt less like the result of a frantic search for valuables and more like a deliberate staging. The killer hadn't just taken a life; they had curated the scene of their passing. This same unsettling order had been present at the deaths of Ramiro Diaz and Frank Kowalski. No ransacking, no wanton destruction. Just the clean, precise end.

Captain Davies had assigned a task force to the recent spate of murders, a predictable response to public pressure. Gwen, however, found herself working on the periphery, her official duties keeping her tethered to the more mundane aspects of police work. But her mind was a million miles away, replaying the details of each case, searching for the invisible threads that bound them together. She found herself returning to Michael's file with an almost obsessive regularity. Vance had closed the case, labeling it a tragic but ultimately random act of violence, a statistic in the city's grim tally. But Gwen had always known, with a certainty that gnawed at her soul, that it was more. There had been a coldness to it, a disturbing lack of frenzy that spoke of something far more deliberate than a street mugging gone wrong.

She remembered Michael's fascination with the intricacies of criminal psychology, his late-night hours spent poring over case files, his almost academic interest in the minds of murderers. He had a theory that every killer, no matter how chaotic their actions might seem, operated within a framework of logic, a personal set of rules that governed their behavior. "You have to think like them, Gwen," he'd told her once, his eyes bright with an almost feverish intensity. "You have to understand their obsession, their compulsion, their unique way of seeing the world." At the time, she'd indulged his enthusiasm, but now, those words echoed with a chilling resonance.

The indigo fiber. The precision. The absence of struggle. The staged cleanliness of the crime scenes. These were not the hallmarks of a common criminal. They suggested a planner, a strategist, someone who approached murder not as an act of passion, but as a meticulously executed operation. And the chilling realization that this same level of calculated control might have been at play in Michael's death was almost unbearable. It transformed the grief she carried into a raw, burning urgency. She wasn't just seeking justice for Ramiro, Frank, and Sarah; she was seeking an answer to the question that had haunted her for years.

Gwen pushed aside the official reports and pulled out a worn notebook, its pages filled with her own scrawled observations and theories. She sketched out the known details of each murder, trying to visualize the connections. Ramiro, the quiet corner store owner. Frank, the burly dockworker. Sarah, the bright young analyst. Their lives intersected only in their brutal, untimely ends. But the *how* of their deaths was the common denominator, the chillingly elegant signature that linked them. A single, precise wound. A targeted strike. An almost surgical removal of life.

She remembered Michael's own death – a single gunshot, precisely placed. No signs of a struggle, no forced entry into his apartment. The weapon had never been found. Vance had dismissed it as a professional hit, but even then, Gwen had felt a nagging dissonance. There had been something too personal, too... intimate about the violence. Or perhaps, too impersonal. A chilling disconnect between the act and any discernible motive.

The indigo fiber became her anchor, a tangible piece of evidence that refused to be dismissed. She'd spent countless hours since Michael's death revisiting his crime scene, her mind replaying every detail, searching for anything, any anomaly that might have been missed. The fiber was one such anomaly. A fleeting detail, logged and filed away, deemed too insignificant to pursue. But now, in the context of these new murders, it felt like a beacon in the darkness.

She began to meticulously re-examine the files of the recent victims, not for new evidence, but for familiar echoes. She looked at the initial responding officers' reports, the forensic notes, the preliminary witness statements – anything that might have been overlooked or dismissed as irrelevant. She was searching for the ghost of a pattern, the phantom limb of a larger design.

The convenience store's security footage, though grainy and unreliable, had shown Ramiro's final moments. A shadow, a flicker of movement, and then nothing. It was as if the killer had ghosted through the frame, leaving no discernible trace. The dockyard had offered no witnesses, only the lingering scent of diesel and the mournful cry of gulls. Sarah's attack had occurred in a blind spot, a notorious gap in the otherwise omnipresent surveillance of the financial district. This wasn't the work of a desperate opportunist. This was a predator who understood the city's rhythms, its vulnerabilities, its blind spots.

Gwen felt a tremor run through her, not of fear, but of a grim, dawning understanding. The killer wasn't just efficient; they were intelligent. They were careful. They were methodical. And the methods, the chilling echoes of Michael's case, were no longer subtle suggestions but glaring accusations. The weight of justice denied, for her brother and for the lives recently extinguished, pressed down on her with an almost physical force. The city was afraid, but Gwen was entering a different kind of terror – the terrifying realization that the shadows held not just random monsters, but a calculating mind, a mind that might just be orchestrating a symphony of death, with her brother's murder as its opening, chilling prelude. She knew, with a certainty that chilled her to the bone, that she had to follow the indigo thread, no matter where it led, for the sake of all the lives that had been unjustly extinguished, and for the truth that had been buried for too long. The ghosts of the past were not just memories; they were harbingers of present terrors, and they were whispering a name that Gwen was beginning to fear she would have to confront.

Chapter 3: The Puppeteer's First Moves

The hum of the city, a constant, low thrum beneath the surface of everyday life, had always been a source of distant comfort to Adam. It was a testament to the countless individual dramas playing out simultaneously, each a tiny, self-contained universe of hopes, fears, and routines. Tonight, however, the symphony of the mundane felt different. It was no longer background noise; it was a vast, intricate network of potential players, each one a piece waiting to be moved on his meticulously crafted board. He sat in his sterile, minimalist apartment, the city lights painting geometric patterns across the polished concrete floor, a stark contrast to the chaotic vibrancy outside. His gaze, usually fixed on the esoteric texts that lined his walls or the complex algorithms that danced across his monitors, now swept over the digital projections of his surveillance feeds, searching for a specific kind of resonance.

He was not looking for the obviously broken, the ones already teetering on the precipice. Those were too easy, too predictable. The thrill, the true artistry, lay in the dismantling of perceived strength, the subtle unraveling of contentment, the precise application of pressure until even the most robust structure fractured. He sought the illusion of perfection, the veneer of effortless success, the individual who believed themselves immune to the insidious currents that Adam understood so intimately. They were the ones who would provide the most spectacular fall, the most devastating ripple effect.

His current obsession, the nascent stage of his next intricate design, centered on a woman named Eleanor Vance. The name itself held a certain resonance, a subtle echo of a past he had long since purged from his conscious memory, yet which still, in oblique ways, informed his actions. Eleanor Vance. Not *the* Vance, of course. The latter was a brute, a blunt instrument, easily understood and ultimately, predictably, contained. This Eleanor was different. She was a curator, a tastemaker, a woman who sculpted beauty from the ephemeral – art, experiences, social connections. Her digital footprint was a meticulously curated garden, each post, each interaction, a carefully placed bloom designed to showcase a life of refined taste and effortless grace.

Adam had spent weeks, perhaps months, in the periphery of her existence, a digital phantom observing her carefully constructed reality. He'd traced her through encrypted social media accounts, anonymized online purchases, and the labyrinthine trails left by her various digital interactions. He knew her preferred artisanal coffee shops, the gallery openings she frequented, the exclusive clubs she belonged to. He knew the subtle nuances of her laughter, captured in leaked event recordings, the way her eyes crinkled at the corners when she was genuinely amused, a rare vulnerability he cataloged with detached fascination. He knew her public persona was a masterpiece of calculated presentation, a carefully woven tapestry of elegance and sophistication.

Her husband, Captain Vance, was a ghost in her digital narrative, a tangential figure mentioned in passing, always framed within the context of his demanding career. Adam had observed Vance's brief appearances in Eleanor's carefully constructed online life with a mixture of disdain and a grudging respect for the woman's ability to compartmentalize. Vance, with his gruff pronouncements and predictable, heavy-handed methods, was a creature of the established order, a man who dealt in the tangible, the observable. He was a stark contrast to Eleanor, who trafficked in the abstract, the emotional, the aesthetically pleasing. And it was this very contrast that made her such a compelling subject.

Adam meticulously reviewed the data streams, his fingers dancing across the holographic interface. Eleanor Vance, at 38, was the picture of affluent success. Co-founder of a successful art consultancy firm, she navigated the city's elite social circles with an ease that suggested a lifetime of ingrained privilege. Her digital life painted a portrait of a woman utterly in control, surrounded by beauty, admired by many, seemingly untouched by the harsh realities that Adam found so endlessly fascinating. Her Instagram feed was a testament to her curated perfection: sun-drenched vacations, perfectly plated meals, art installations that spoke of both intellectual prowess and a keen aesthetic sensibility. There were no outward signs of stress, no hints of the cracks that Adam knew lay hidden beneath the polished surface of every human being.

He paused, his gaze sharpening on a particular set of data. Eleanor Vance. The name itself, a phantom limb reaching out from his own forgotten past. A flicker, so faint it could have been a glitch in the system, registered in the deep recesses of his mind. He dismissed it. He did not allow sentimentality to cloud his judgment. This was not personal. It was an equation, a carefully balanced system of variables, and Eleanor Vance was simply the most intriguing unknown.

His selection process was a clinical dissection. He analyzed her social network, not for its size or reach, but for its composition. He mapped her key relationships – the confidantes, the rivals, the admirers. He noted the subtle shifts in her interactions, the unspoken tensions, the dependencies. He cross-referenced her digital presence with the more mundane data points he'd gathered: financial records, property deeds, travel itineraries. He was building a multidimensional model of her existence, looking for the points of leverage, the hidden fault lines.

He found her to be deeply rooted in her social ecosystem. Her friendships, though seemingly robust, were predicated on shared experiences and aesthetic alignment rather than profound emotional connection. There was a subtle undercurrent of competition, a unspoken jockeying for position that was evident in the carefully worded compliments and the subtly veiled critiques that peppered her online interactions. This was fertile ground. A person whose sense of self was so intrinsically linked to external validation and social standing was inherently vulnerable. A disruption to that carefully constructed image would be devastating.

Adam's attention shifted to her professional life. Her art consultancy firm, "Lumière & Hue," was more than just a business; it was an extension of her identity. She cultivated an image of discerning taste and impeccable judgment. Her clients were the city's wealthy elite, individuals who sought not just art, but a statement, a reflection of their own status and sophistication. Adam noted the high stakes involved in these transactions, the immense sums of money, the delicate egos involved. Any perceived lapse in judgment, any public scandal, would not only damage her reputation but could potentially cripple her business.

He zoomed in on a particular transaction, a significant acquisition for a notoriously demanding client. The details were sparse in the public domain, but Adam's access was not so limited. He saw the intricate negotiations, the subtle pressures, the potential for misstep. He observed Eleanor's meticulous attention to detail, her confident assertiveness in navigating the complex landscape of high-end art acquisition. It was impressive, in its way. But it was also a façade. Beneath the veneer of control, Adam sensed the subtle anxieties, the constant pressure to maintain her flawless record.

He contrasted her public life with the few glimpses he could find of her private moments. She appeared to be a woman who valued order and beauty above all else. Her apartment, when seen in fleeting glimpses through carefully staged social media posts, was a sanctuary of minimalist design, devoid of clutter or extraneous ornamentation. It was a space that reflected her desire for control, her need for a serene environment. This starkly contrasted with the chaotic, often messy, nature of human emotion, a realm Adam understood intimately.

Adam's mind, a finely tuned instrument of analysis, began to construct the framework for his next "game." Eleanor Vance was not a victim of circumstance. She was a willing participant in a carefully constructed reality, a reality that Adam was uniquely equipped to deconstruct. Her perceived strength – her social grace, her professional acumen, her seemingly effortless command of her environment – were precisely the attributes that would make her downfall so profound. She was the embodiment of the superficial order that Adam found so contemptible, and so ripe for disruption.

He initiated a new series of digital probes, each one a precisely calibrated whisper designed to sow discord. He didn't seek to harm her physically, not directly. His artistry lay in the psychological. He aimed to erode her confidence, to introduce doubt, to turn her meticulously crafted world against her. He began with the subtle manipulation of information, the gentle nudging of digital currents. Small anomalies would appear in her online accounts, minor glitches in her financial records, carefully placed rumors that would insinuate themselves into the periphery of her carefully guarded social circles.

He imagined her reaction, the initial dismissal, the slight prickle of unease. He pictured her seeking explanations, finding none that satisfied. He envisioned the seed of doubt taking root, growing in the fertile soil of her need for perfection. She would begin to question her own judgment, her own perception of reality. The confidence that served as her armor would begin to chip away, revealing the anxieties that lay beneath.

Adam was not driven by malice, but by a profound, almost philosophical, dissatisfaction with the perceived order of the world. He saw the superficiality, the pretense, the carefully constructed illusions that people clung to. He believed that true understanding, true liberation, came from confronting the chaos within, from acknowledging the fragility of the human psyche. His games were not acts of cruelty; they were elaborate, high-stakes experiments in existential deconstruction.

He had chosen Eleanor Vance not because she was weak, but because she was a meticulously crafted symbol of a world he sought to expose. Her social standing, her professional success, her apparent contentment – these were the very qualities that made her an ideal canvas for his art. The more perfect the façade, the more spectacular the collapse. The stakes were high, not just for Eleanor, but for Adam himself. Each move, each calculated step, was a testament to his own intricate understanding of the human condition, a demonstration of his mastery over the invisible forces that governed desire, fear, and the desperate need for control. The city, with its millions of untold stories, had just provided him with his next, most compelling narrative. The stage was set, and the puppeteer was ready to begin his delicate dance.

The first tendrils of Adam's influence were not a storm, but a gentle, almost imperceptible shift in the breeze. He understood that the most effective infiltration was not through brute force, but through the insidious creep of familiarity, the slow erosion of boundaries disguised as serendipity. Eleanor Vance, with her carefully curated existence, was a fortress built on layers of sophisticated defenses. To breach it, he needed a skeleton key, a method that would unlock her trust without triggering alarm.

His initial forays were masked by the anonymity of the digital ether, a realm where he was a ghost in the machine, observing and cataloging. He had meticulously mapped her social landscape, identifying the common threads that bound her to her select circle. One such thread was her patronage of a particular avant-garde gallery on the Lower East Side, a space known for its daring exhibitions and its discerning clientele. Adam, through a series of untraceable transactions and the careful manipulation of a shell corporation, became a temporary patron himself, a silent investor who had recently acquired a significant stake in the gallery.

His presence was announced not through direct introduction, but through subtle operational adjustments. A new, more sophisticated security system was installed, implemented by a discreet, highly skilled firm Adam had vetted. He anonymously funded a small, exclusive event – a private viewing of a provocative new installation by an artist Eleanor had publicly praised in a recently published interview. The invitations were distributed selectively, ensuring that only those with a genuine appreciation for the artist's work, and by extension, Eleanor's taste, would attend. Adam himself was not present, not yet. He was the unseen hand guiding the currents, creating the conditions for a carefully orchestrated encounter.

Eleanor arrived, as expected, a vision of understated elegance. Adam had studied her sartorial choices, her preferred designers, the subtle nuances of her aesthetic. He knew she gravitated towards clean lines, luxurious fabrics, and a palette of muted, sophisticated tones. The gallery, under his silent influence, had been subtly reconfigured. The lighting was adjusted to highlight the very pieces Eleanor had recently admired in that interview, creating an almost personalized experience for her. The air hummed with a carefully curated soundtrack, a blend of ambient electronica and classical pieces he knew she favored.

He had, through his digital reconnaissance, identified a point of minor friction in her professional life: a potential acquisition of a rare piece of early Renaissance sculpture that had been proving elusive. He had also noted her frustration, subtly expressed in a private message to a close confidante that had been intercepted and analyzed. The sculpture, a small but historically significant work, was rumored to be in the possession of a private collector known for his reclusiveness and his rather eccentric negotiation tactics. This collector was, by chance, also a known, albeit distant, associate of a major benefactor who had recently made a substantial donation to the gallery – a donation facilitated, in part, by Adam's shell corporation.

Adam orchestrated a subtle reveal. He arranged for a discreet note, penned in elegant calligraphy on thick, cream-colored stationery, to be slipped into Eleanor's coat pocket as she admired a particularly striking piece. The note contained no identifying information, only a cryptic message: "The Gryphon sleeps in shadow. Its keeper guards its slumber with a formidable will, but even the most vigilant eye can be persuaded by a shared appreciation for the truly sublime. The Louvre holds a mirror to its soul." It was a riddle, designed to pique her intellectual curiosity, to tap into her love for esoteric knowledge and veiled allusions, a known characteristic he'd gleaned from her online musings on art history.

He waited. He knew the note would intrigue her, perhaps even frustrate her. He observed through his remote feeds as she reread the message, her brow furrowed in concentration, a rare moment of public uncertainty that Adam found immensely satisfying. He watched as she subtly showed it to her companion, a fellow art connoisseur, and observed their shared speculation. The seed was planted.

Days later, Adam made his first physical move, disguised as an accidental encounter. He frequented a small, independent bookstore nestled in a quiet corner of the West Village, a place known for its rare art books and its knowledgeable proprietor. He knew Eleanor occasionally visited this establishment, drawn by its curated selection and its hushed atmosphere. He positioned himself near a shelf dedicated to Renaissance sculpture, a copy of a well-regarded monograph open in his hands. He was not engrossed in the text, but strategically placed, his posture conveying an air of quiet contemplation.

As Eleanor entered, he feigned a slight startle, his eyes meeting hers for a brief, polite moment. He offered a faint, apologetic smile, a gesture of gentlemanly deference. He made no attempt to engage her directly, but as she passed, he allowed the monograph to slip from his grasp, its pages fanning open to a detailed illustration of the very

Gryphon sculpture he had alluded to in his note.

He bent to retrieve it, his movements slow and deliberate. Eleanor, her curiosity piqued by the earlier note and now confronted with this visual echo, paused. Her eyes lingered on the illustration, then flickered to his face. Adam met her gaze, a subtle warmth in his expression. "Forgive me," he murmured, his voice a low, resonant baritone, carefully modulated for an impression of thoughtful sincerity. "I'm afraid my fascination with this particular piece tends to make me... clumsy."

He held the book up slightly, allowing her a clearer view. "The Gryphon of Verona," he continued, his tone conversational, as if sharing a casual observation. "A truly remarkable artifact. Such exquisite detail in the musculature, and the gaze... there's a profound melancholy captured in stone, wouldn't you agree?"

He watched her reaction. He saw the flicker of recognition, the subtle tightening of her jaw that indicated she was connecting the illustration to his earlier cryptic message. He offered a gentle, disarming smile. "It's said that the sculptor infused it with the sorrow of a lost love. A rather romantic notion, perhaps, but one that resonates when you consider the piece in person."

He was offering her a shared intellectual space, a common ground based on a mutual appreciation for art and its hidden narratives. He was not asking for anything, not probing for personal details, simply sharing a passion. This was the first, crucial step: establishing a veneer of shared interest, of intellectual kinship.

Eleanor, after a moment of hesitation, responded. Her voice was as polished as her public image, but with a subtle warmth that Adam had noted in rare, unguarded moments. "Indeed," she replied, her gaze still fixed on the illustration. "The legend is quite compelling. I've been... researching it recently."

Adam inclined his head, a gesture of respect. "Ah, then you'll understand my rather unprofessional clumsiness. It's a piece that commands attention, even in a book." He paused, allowing the silence to hang, not uncomfortably, but expectantly. "I confess," he added, a touch of vulnerability in his tone, "I've always been drawn to artifacts with stories etched into their very being. The tangible remnants of human passion, of joy and sorrow."

He was carefully weaving a narrative for himself, a persona of a fellow enthusiast, a kindred spirit. He was projecting an image of someone who understood the deeper resonance of art, someone who shared Eleanor’s own perceived sensibility. He saw the subtle relaxation in her posture, the way her initial reserve began to soften. He had successfully navigated the first hurdle, moving from an unseen observer to a potential acquaintance, a fellow traveler on the artistic landscape.

He didn't press further. He simply offered a polite nod. "It was a pleasure to share the moment," he said, his voice carrying a hint of regret, as if genuinely disappointed that the encounter was ending. He then turned back to the book, allowing her the space to move on. He watched from his peripheral vision as she continued through the bookstore, her pace slightly more animated than before. He had not acquired intimate details, not yet. But he had gained something more valuable: a crack in her carefully constructed detachment, a flicker of curiosity directed at him. He had initiated a conversation, albeit one veiled in art and circumstance, and he was confident that Eleanor Vance, in her pursuit of the sublime, would seek out the source of that intriguing whisper. The infiltration had begun, not with a bang, but with the soft rustle of pages, a shared glance, and a whispered legend. He had offered her a tantalizing piece of the puzzle, and he knew, with absolute certainty, that she would want to solve it. The subtle manipulation of perceived coincidence was his forte, and he was just beginning to play his hand.

The subtle dance Adam performed with Eleanor Vance was a masterpiece of psychological manipulation, a carefully choreographed waltz where every step was calculated to foster a growing sense of unease. He understood that true power lay not in overt force, but in the insidious unraveling of a person's reality, the slow erosion of their certainty until they questioned everything and everyone around them. The previous encounter in the bookstore had been the initial spark, a carefully manufactured moment of serendipity designed to pique her intellectual curiosity. Now, the embers needed to be fanned, not into a blaze of suspicion, but into a persistent, low-grade fever of doubt.

His strategy was multifaceted, targeting not just Eleanor's internal state but also her external world. He began by leveraging the information gleaned from her intercepted communications, those seemingly innocuous exchanges with friends and colleagues that painted a picture of her vulnerabilities and insecurities. He knew, for instance, that Eleanor prided herself on her sharp intuition, her ability to discern authenticity and to navigate complex social dynamics with grace. This very strength, Adam decided, would be his primary weapon against her.

He started with subtle, almost imperceptible drifts in her professional sphere. A rumor, carefully seeded through an anonymous email to a trusted associate of

Eleanor's, suggested a competitor was subtly undermining her position on a prestigious art acquisition committee. The email was vague, couched in terms of concern rather than accusation, mentioning "unusual behind-the-scenes maneuvering" and hinting at "a carefully crafted narrative designed to cast shadows on certain decisions." It was designed to sound like insider gossip, a well-intentioned warning from someone who valued Eleanor's integrity. The source was untraceable, a phantom email address created through a convoluted series of VPNs and disposable accounts, a digital wraith leaving no trace.

Adam's involvement with the gallery also provided a fertile ground for sowing discord. He had observed Eleanor's interactions with Marcus Thorne, a fellow patron and a man of considerable influence within the art world. While their relationship appeared cordial, Adam had detected a subtle undercurrent of professional rivalry, a silent competition for influence and access. Using a proxy account – a persona he had meticulously constructed online as a burgeoning art critic with a penchant for unearthing inconvenient truths – Adam began to post veiled criticisms of Thorne's recent acquisitions, framing them as either aesthetically questionable or ethically dubious. These posts were designed to resonate with Eleanor's own discerning eye and her known disdain for ostentatious displays of wealth without substance.

He escalated this by subtly altering the context of conversations. During a charity auction Eleanor was attending, Adam, present under a different guise as a wealthy, anonymous donor, arranged for a strategically placed phone call. His associate, privy to Adam's instructions, made a public, albeit hushed, inquiry to a mutual acquaintance of Eleanor and Thorne about "Thorne's latest acquisition of the Medici cameo." The question was framed as one of genuine interest, but the tone, amplified by the auction house's hushed atmosphere, carried a subtle implication of something being amiss. The intention was for the comment to reach Eleanor, to create a tiny fissure in her perception of Thorne's unimpeachable reputation. Adam watched from a distance, a ghost in the opulent ballroom, as Eleanor's brow furrowed almost imperceptibly. He knew the seed of doubt, however small, had been sown.

The digital realm, his primary hunting ground, was where Adam truly excelled in the art of planting seeds of doubt. He had access to Eleanor's cloud storage, a vault of her professional correspondence and personal notes. He didn't need to fabricate anything outright; the truth, strategically presented, was far more potent. He discovered an exchange where Eleanor expressed mild frustration with her financial advisor over a perceived oversight regarding a tax deduction for a recent art purchase. Adam meticulously altered a single sentence in one of Eleanor's outgoing emails, subtly changing the tone from mild annoyance to one of outright distrust and accusation. He then ensured this subtly altered email found its way to the advisor's inbox, not directly from Eleanor, but through a "forwarded chain" that appeared to originate from a disgruntled former client of the advisor, adding an air of corroborating evidence. The aim was not to destroy the relationship, but to introduce a persistent prickle of anxiety, a nagging question about the competence and trustworthiness of someone Eleanor relied upon.

He also understood the power of shared experience, even if that experience was fabricated. He knew Eleanor's circle valued discretion and loyalty. He identified a woman, Amelia Hayes, a seemingly loyal friend and confidante of Eleanor, whose online presence revealed a mild dissatisfaction with her own professional trajectory and a subtle envy of Eleanor's success. Adam initiated contact with Amelia through a burner social media profile, posing as a former colleague of hers from years ago. He began to subtly feed her information, seemingly innocuous observations about Eleanor's recent successes, framed with a feigned admiration that masked a more insidious agenda. He would mention, in passing, how Eleanor had secured a particular commission that Amelia had also expressed interest in, or how Eleanor's name was being consistently put forward for opportunities Amelia felt she deserved.

He never directly asked Amelia to betray Eleanor. Instead, he cultivated a narrative that suggested Eleanor was benefiting from circumstances Amelia was being denied, subtly amplifying Amelia's existing insecurities. He would pose hypothetical questions, such as, "It's amazing how Eleanor always seems to be in the right place at the right time. Do you think it's pure luck, or something more... strategic?" These were designed to plant the idea in Amelia's mind, to make her look for patterns of advantage, to question the fairness of Eleanor's ascent. Adam meticulously monitored Amelia's responses, her subtle shifts in tone, her growing engagement with his manufactured narrative. He was patiently nurturing a fragile ecosystem of suspicion, waiting for the right moment to introduce a catalyst.

The catalyst came in the form of a "chance" encounter. Adam orchestrated a situation where he, as his anonymous art critic persona, was overheard by Amelia, while she was with a mutual acquaintance of Eleanor's, discussing a supposed discrepancy in the provenance of a piece Eleanor had recently authenticated. The conversation was designed to sound like a professional debate, but the choice of words was deliberately ambiguous, hinting at a lack of thoroughness on Eleanor's part. He made sure the specific artwork was one Eleanor had publicly championed, making the implied criticism all the more pointed. He saw Amelia's eyes widen, her posture stiffen. He knew she would relay this information, perhaps even embellish it, to Eleanor, or worse, to others who might doubt Eleanor's judgment.

Adam's methods were not about grand gestures. They were about the persistent drip, drip, drip of uncertainty. He understood that a human mind, particularly one accustomed to order and logic, could be profoundly destabilized by even the slightest suggestion that its own perceptions were flawed. He manufactured misunderstandings between Eleanor and her colleagues, subtly altering the tone of emails or misrepresenting statements made in casual conversation. A brief, friendly remark from Eleanor about a colleague's new project might be relayed by Adam's proxy as a thinly veiled criticism of its artistic merit, complete with an exaggerated sigh and an eye-roll. The recipient would then approach Eleanor with a defensive posture, creating an awkward tension that had no discernible origin for Eleanor herself.

He also played on Eleanor's fear of professional isolation. He knew she valued her reputation for integrity. He began to subtly isolate her from her support network. He would intercept communications between Eleanor and her closest confidantes, planting seeds of discord. He might forward a private message from a friend to Eleanor that, when viewed in isolation, seemed dismissive of Eleanor's recent anxieties, implying that her worries were unfounded or even self-indulgent. Conversely, he might subtly alter a message from Eleanor to a friend, making it sound more demanding or critical than intended, leading the friend to feel resentful or misunderstood.

The goal was never overt destruction, but a gradual, almost imperceptible erosion of trust. Adam wanted Eleanor to begin to second-guess her own judgment, to doubt the sincerity of those around her, and ultimately, to question the stability of her own reality. He was the unseen puppeteer, his strings invisible, his movements precise. Each action, each carefully placed word, each manufactured coincidence, was a step in a grand design to unravel Eleanor Vance, not by breaking her, but by convincing her that she was already broken. He was planting seeds of doubt, and he was a patient gardener, knowing that with time and meticulous cultivation, they would inevitably blossom into a suffocating harvest of uncertainty. He watched her through the digital veil, observing the subtle shifts in her online interactions, the hesitations, the moments of prolonged silence that indicated a mind grappling with unseen pressures. The game had just begun, and the first, crucial phase of destabilization was well underway.

Adam understood that the most potent poison was often administered in the smallest, most undetectable doses. He had meticulously laid the groundwork, subtly chipping away at Eleanor's sense of certainty, making her question her own perceptions. Now, the time had come to sever the anchors that tethered her to reality, to isolate her in the echoing chambers of her own mind. His strategy was no longer about planting seeds of doubt; it was about cultivating a wilderness of suspicion, where every friendly face would appear as a potential adversary, and every comforting word would sound like a veiled threat.

The first tendril of this isolation reached out towards Eleanor's most trusted confidante, Sarah Jenkins. Sarah, a pragmatic and grounded individual, was Eleanor's sounding board, the one person who consistently offered an anchor of reason amidst Eleanor's more introspective tendencies. Adam's objective: to paint Sarah as an unreliable friend, subtly implying a betrayal of confidence. He achieved this by exploiting a minor indiscretion from Sarah's past, a brief period of professional recklessness that, while long forgiven by Eleanor, had left a lingering shadow of guilt.

Adam, operating through a series of anonymized digital personas, began a campaign of targeted 'leaks.' He anonymously forwarded a heavily redacted email thread from Sarah's personal archive to a mutual acquaintance of Eleanor's, one who possessed a particular penchant for gossip. The emails, taken out of context, suggested Sarah had shared sensitive information about Eleanor's personal struggles with a third party, framing it as casual gossip rather than a moment of seeking advice. The forwarded message was accompanied by a brief, chilling note: "Some friends are not as loyal as they seem. Be careful who you trust." The recipient, predictably, wasted no time in relaying this 'information' back to Eleanor, couched in concerned whispers about Sarah's questionable discretion.

Eleanor, already conditioned by Adam's subtle manipulations to be wary, found herself thrown into a vortex of conflicting emotions. She valued Sarah's friendship immensely, but the evidence, however circumstantial, gnawed at her. She recalled a moment, weeks prior, where Sarah had alluded to having overheard something concerning Eleanor's project at the gallery. At the time, Eleanor had dismissed it as Sarah being overly cautious. Now, the memory resurfaced with a venomous clarity, twisted by the anonymous message into a potential breach of trust.

Adam didn't stop there. He escalated his efforts by creating a scenario where Eleanor's perception of Sarah's intentions would be irrevocably skewed. He orchestrated a "chance" encounter between Sarah and a disreputable art dealer, a man known for his predatory practices, whom Eleanor had explicitly warned Sarah to avoid. Adam, using a carefully constructed online profile as a wealthy collector, made sure to be present at the same upscale gallery event where Sarah was also in attendance. He subtly guided the conversation, using a proxy to engage Sarah in a discussion about a specific, highly sought-after piece that Eleanor had been pursuing. During this exchange, Adam "casually" mentioned to a nearby acquaintance, loud enough for Eleanor to overhear, his surprise at Sarah's "audacity" in speaking with the disreputable dealer about such a valuable acquisition, implying Sarah was either ignorant of the dealer's true nature or, worse, attempting to circumvent Eleanor.

Eleanor, observing from across the room, saw Sarah speaking animatedly with the dealer. The anonymous email, the 'overheard' conversation, and now this seemingly public endorsement of Sarah's association with a shady character – it all coalesced into a damning picture. Her mind, already predisposed to doubt, seized upon this as confirmation of Sarah's duplicity. She retreated, her heart a leaden weight in her chest, the warmth of friendship replaced by the icy tendrils of suspicion. She withdrew from Sarah, her calls unanswered, her messages left unread. The silence that followed was deafening, a void created by Adam's meticulous machinations.

The isolation wasn't confined to Eleanor's personal relationships; it permeated her professional life as well. Adam targeted her esteemed mentor, Professor Alistair Finch. Finch was a pillar of intellectual integrity, a man whose opinion Eleanor deeply respected. Adam understood that undermining this relationship would not only isolate Eleanor but also cast a shadow over her professional credibility.

Adam initiated a sophisticated disinformation campaign targeting Finch. He fabricated a series of online articles and blog posts, written under the guise of disgruntled academics, that subtly critiqued Finch's earlier seminal work on Renaissance art theory. These pieces didn't outright attack Finch, but rather, they posed hypothetical scenarios that cast doubt on the foundational premises of his research, hinting at overlooked evidence or biased interpretations. The articles were subtly linked to Eleanor's own published essays, creating a spurious connection that suggested she was either attempting to usurp Finch's legacy or, more insidiously, that her work was being influenced by flawed theories that were now coming to light.

Furthermore, Adam used his access to gallery correspondence to subtly alter the tone of Eleanor's communications with Finch. He would insert phrases that, out of context, could be interpreted as condescending or overly critical of Finch's recent contributions to the field. For instance, a carefully worded acknowledgment of Finch's latest publication might be subtly tweaked to sound patronizing, with a phrase like, "While I appreciate your... *efforts* to revisit the topic, I believe my own research presents a more *nuanced* perspective," replacing a more deferential tone. He ensured these altered messages were sent from Eleanor's account, disguised as minor typos or autocorrect errors that had slipped through, plausible deniability being paramount.

Professor Finch, a man of routine and deeply rooted in his established theories, began to feel a growing disquiet. He noticed the subtle shift in Eleanor's tone, the veiled criticisms that seemed to appear with increasing frequency. He also encountered the fabricated articles, their intellectual veneer making them difficult to dismiss outright. He began to question Eleanor's judgment, her respect for his work, and her true intentions. Their once vibrant intellectual exchange began to dwindle, replaced by a cautious, almost adversarial politeness. Eleanor, sensing Finch's withdrawal, felt a profound sense of professional abandonment. The esteemed mentor she had always relied on for guidance now seemed distant, his gaze tinged with skepticism. She was adrift in her own field, her intellectual compass spinning wildly.

Adam's strategy was to create a domino effect. The isolation from Sarah weakened Eleanor's emotional support system, making her more susceptible to professional anxieties. The perceived disapproval of Professor Finch amplified these anxieties, leading her to question her own capabilities. With her closest friend alienated and her mentor's respect seemingly lost, Eleanor was increasingly alone, her world shrinking with each passing day.

The final, crucial step in this phase was to isolate Eleanor from any external validation, any source of objective truth that could counter Adam's narrative. He targeted her work directly, not by sabotaging it, but by subtly undermining its context and reception. He learned, through her private communications, about a significant upcoming exhibition she was curating, one that held immense potential for her career. He identified a rival curator, a man named Julian Croft, known for his ambition and his less-than-ethical methods.

Adam began to sow seeds of discord between Eleanor and Croft. He anonymously leaked fabricated information to Croft about Eleanor's exhibition, suggesting that Eleanor was attempting to steal certain artistic concepts or interpretations that Croft had been developing for his own upcoming shows. This was achieved by creating a series of "anonymous tips" sent to Croft's professional email, filled with misleading details about Eleanor's research and artist consultations. These tips were designed to paint Eleanor as a manipulative and opportunistic figure.

Simultaneously, Adam intervened in the public sphere, manipulating online discourse surrounding the art world. He orchestrated a campaign on art-focused forums and social media platforms, using multiple sock-puppet accounts to generate negative buzz about Eleanor's upcoming exhibition. These accounts would post thinly veiled criticisms, questioning the originality of her chosen artists, hinting at conflicts of interest in her acquisitions, and even suggesting a lack of genuine artistic merit in her curatorial vision. The language used was carefully calibrated to mimic genuine art critique, making it difficult for casual observers to discern the manufactured nature of the negativity. Phrases like "a predictable collection," "lacking in intellectual depth," and "uninspired choices" began to circulate, creating a cloud of doubt before the exhibition even opened.

Adam also subtly manipulated the flow of information to art critics who were scheduled to review Eleanor's exhibition. He ensured that their pre-exhibition briefings were subtly skewed, perhaps by anonymously sending them fabricated research papers that cast doubt on the historical significance of the artists Eleanor was featuring, or by circulating a fabricated rumor about a scandal involving one of the featured artists. The goal was to ensure that these critics, when they arrived at the exhibition, would be predisposed to view the work through a lens of skepticism, actively searching for flaws rather than celebrating achievements.

Eleanor, already feeling the sting of her fractured personal relationships, began to notice the growing chorus of online negativity. She saw the whispers of doubt about her exhibition, the subtle criticisms in art forums, and the unsettling lack of enthusiastic previews from the art press. She felt an overwhelming sense of being undermined, of her hard work being met with a pervasive, almost conspiratorial, disapproval. The isolation was complete. Sarah was a ghost. Finch was a stranger. And the art world, her sanctuary, seemed to be turning against her. She was trapped in a labyrinth of her own making, a prison constructed brick by brick by Adam, the unseen architect of her despair. He watched her digital footprint, noting the increased searches for terms like "professional betrayal," "loss of confidence," and "imposter syndrome." The harvest of isolation was beginning to ripen. He had successfully stripped away her support systems, her professional validation, and her sense of belonging. She was now a solitary figure, her gaze turned inward, vulnerable and ready for the next phase of his insidious game. The silence around her was not merely an absence of sound; it was a suffocating weight, a testament to his triumph in dismantling her world, piece by agonizing piece. She was adrift, a ship with no sails, no rudder, and no harbor in sight, entirely at the mercy of the currents Adam had so masterfully orchestrated.

The silence that had descended between Eleanor and Sarah was a chasm, growing wider with each unanswered call and unread text. Eleanor found herself staring at her phone for hours, the glowing screen a stark testament to her isolation. Each unread message was a fresh barb, reinforcing the anonymous whispers and Adam's orchestrated encounters. The pragmatism that Sarah had always embodied now seemed to her like a calculated deception, her once reliable counsel a carefully constructed performance. Eleanor replayed their last conversation, searching for any hint of insincerity, any flicker of falsehood in Sarah's eyes. Had Sarah's concerned inquiries about her project always been a subtle probing, a gathering of ammunition? The gallery event replayed in her mind with agonizing clarity: Sarah, animatedly talking to the disreputable dealer, while Eleanor watched from afar, a knot of dread tightening in her stomach. The pitying glances from acquaintances now seemed like shared secrets, an unspoken understanding of Sarah's perfidy. Eleanor began to avoid even casual encounters, fearing that any interaction would expose her vulnerability, that the phantom whispers would coalesce into tangible accusations.

Professor Finch's gradual withdrawal was equally unsettling. Their intellectual sparring, once a source of invigorating debate and mutual respect, had devolved into stilted pleasantries. Eleanor found herself scrutinizing Finch's every word, every hesitant glance, searching for the disapproval she now felt was so palpable. The fabricated articles, though unsigned and seemingly academic, felt like a targeted assault on her intellect, a posthumous critique of her mentor's life's work, and by extension, her own. She tried to engage him, to rekindle their previous rapport, but her attempts were met with polite evasiveness. Finch, usually so generous with his time and insights, now seemed perpetually occupied, his responses brief and dismissive. Eleanor noticed him looking at her differently, a subtle skepticism in his gaze that chilled her to the bone. Was he questioning her research? Had he indeed found fault with her interpretations, as the anonymous articles suggested? The gnawing uncertainty festered, eroding her confidence in her own scholarly abilities. She began to second-guess her curatorial decisions, her academic instincts, everything she had once held as immutable truths.

The creeping paranoia began to bleed into Eleanor's professional life. The online discourse surrounding her upcoming exhibition, once a source of anticipation, now felt like a hostile environment. The thinly veiled criticisms, the questioning of her choices, the hints of conflict of interest – they all resonated with a terrifying familiarity, echoing the doubts Adam had so meticulously planted. She spent hours sifting through art forums, her heart sinking with each negative comment. She tried to differentiate between genuine critique and manufactured negativity, but the lines had blurred. Was that user genuinely concerned about the originality of the artists, or were they a pawn in a larger game? Was the mention of a scandal involving one of the featured artists a coincidence, or a carefully placed seed of doubt designed to discredit her work? She found herself scrutinizing every art critic's pre-exhibition briefing, searching for any sign of bias, any preconceived notion that could have been influenced by Adam's insidious campaign.

Eleanor's sleep became fragmented, her nights haunted by a pervasive anxiety. She would wake in a cold sweat, convinced she had heard footsteps outside her apartment, or that the shadows in her room held unseen observers. Her appetite waned, and she found herself pacing her apartment for hours, a frantic energy coursing through her veins. The once comforting familiarity of her surroundings now felt alien, charged with a sense of hidden threat. She started to question the security of her own home, checking locks multiple times, peering through the peephole before answering the door. The anonymity of Adam's actions amplified her fear; he was a phantom, an unseen force capable of manipulating her reality from the shadows.

She began to exhibit moments of uncharacteristic impulsivity. During a crucial meeting with potential sponsors for the exhibition, she abruptly launched into a defensive tirade, her voice trembling with an emotion that was clearly out of place. She accused one of the sponsors of having ulterior motives, of not truly understanding the artistic merit of the collection, her words spilling out in a torrent of pent-up anxiety and suspicion. The sponsors, taken aback and clearly unsettled, withdrew their support shortly after. Eleanor, upon reflection, was horrified by her own behavior, but the paranoia had taken root so deeply that she found it difficult to fully regret her outburst. Perhaps they *had* been trying to undermine her, to take advantage of her perceived vulnerability.

Adam observed these changes with a detached fascination, a surgeon meticulously monitoring a patient's vital signs. Eleanor's spiraling anxiety, her erratic behavior, her profound sense of isolation – they were all data points confirming the efficacy of his strategy. He had predicted this descent, had meticulously charted the course from subtle suggestion to outright paranoia. The chasm between her and Sarah, the frostiness of Finch, the poisoned discourse of the art world – these were not mere consequences; they were carefully engineered outcomes. He found a certain grim satisfaction in witnessing her unraveling, in the tangible proof of his control. It was a testament to his intellect, his understanding of human psychology, and his ability to exploit the hidden fault lines within even the most seemingly stable individuals.

He noted the increase in her online searches: "unreliable friends," "professional betrayal," "gaslighting symptoms," "imposter syndrome." These were the hallmarks of his success, the digital footprints of a mind under siege. He saw her increasingly withdrawn online presence, the abrupt cessation of her regular social media updates, the dwindling interactions with her followers. She was withdrawing into herself, her external world shrinking to the confines of her own increasingly fractured perception. The vibrant, confident curator was being replaced by a spectral figure, haunted by unseen forces, her every action dictated by an overwhelming sense of dread.

Eleanor's focus narrowed to an obsessive degree. She began to see conspiracies everywhere. A misplaced file on her desk was not an oversight but a deliberate act of sabotage. A slightly delayed email was a sign that her communications were being intercepted. The familiar faces of her gallery staff, once a source of comfort and support, now seemed to hold an inscrutable distance, their polite smiles masking, she feared, a shared complicity in her downfall. She started to record conversations, to meticulously document every perceived slight, every ambiguous remark, desperate to find concrete proof of the malevolence she sensed all around her.

She developed a particular fixation on Julian Croft, the rival curator. His ambition, which she had once admired with a grudging respect, now appeared as a predatory hunger. She imagined him orchestrating the negative online buzz, feeding information to the critics, and perhaps even influencing Sarah and Finch. The thought that her own professional peers might be actively working against her, with such calculated malice, was almost unbearable. Her grip on reality was loosening, the scaffolding of her former life crumbling around her.

One evening, while reviewing the final layout for the exhibition, a wave of overwhelming despair washed over her. She looked at the meticulously chosen artworks, the catalog she had painstakingly edited, the exhibition notes she had drafted with such care. They all seemed to mock her, to represent a life and a career that was now teetering on the precipice of oblivion. She saw not her achievements, but the specter of their potential failure, the looming shadow of public ridicule and professional ruin. Tears streamed down her face, hot and bitter, as she sank to the floor, the weight of her isolation pressing down on her like a physical force. The carefully constructed façade of her confidence had shattered, revealing the raw, trembling fear beneath. She was adrift in a sea of her own anxieties, the puppeteer's strings taut and invisible, guiding her inexorably towards a predetermined, devastating conclusion. The silence around her was no longer just an absence of sound; it was a deafening roar of her own internal collapse.

Chapter 4: The Investigator's Tightening Net

Gwen's office was a sanctuary of ordered chaos, a testament to her unwavering commitment to untangling the knots of depravity. Stacks of case files, meticulously organized and cross-referenced, rose like miniature skyscrapers on her desk, each one a silent monument to a life cut short. The air hummed with the low thrum of the fluorescent lights and the occasional rustle of paper as she shifted her focus from one tragedy to another. Today, the familiar weight of the files felt heavier, the ghosts within them whispering their unanswered questions. She had been staring at the murder of Elias Thorne for hours, the stark details of the crime scene seared into her memory: the staged disarray, the peculiar placement of the antique clock, the absence of any forced entry. It was a puzzle, and Gwen lived for puzzles, but this one was particularly vexing, its pieces seemingly designed to resist any coherent arrangement.

She'd already exhausted the immediate avenues: the usual suspects, the victim's known associates, the financial records. Thorne, a reclusive horologist with a penchant for antique timepieces, had lived a life as quiet and predictable as the ticking of his beloved clocks. Yet, his end had been anything but. The brutality of the act stood in stark contrast to the placid façade of his existence, a dissonance that gnawed at Gwen. She pushed aside the Thorne file for a moment, her gaze drifting to the case of Clara Bellweather, the renowned but estranged opera singer found dead in her opulent dressing room. The superficial similarities were obvious – the staged scene, the lack of apparent motive – but Gwen believed that true connection lay not in the obvious, but in the subtle, the overlooked.

Her fingers traced the embossed lettering of Clara's file. The singer's life, so public and yet so private, was a complex tapestry of soaring highs and devastating lows. Gwen had interviewed Clara's agent, her vocal coach, her estranged family members, each conversation yielding fragments of a woman consumed by her art and plagued by inner demons. There were whispers of a clandestine affair, of financial pressures, of a deep-seated dissatisfaction that even her prodigious talent couldn't quell. Gwen recalled the agent's nervous fidgeting, the coach's downcast eyes, the terse pronouncements of a sibling who had long since washed his hands of her. Each person had their own narrative, their own biases, their own carefully guarded secrets.

Gwen sighed, leaning back in her chair, the worn leather groaning in protest. The common thread, if one existed, was not a shared enemy or a common debt. It was something far more insidious, something that lurked in the shadows of ordinary lives, waiting for the opportune moment to strike. She picked up a fresh notepad, its pages stark white, a blank canvas for the emerging patterns. Her approach was methodical, almost obsessive. For each victim, she began to construct an intricate timeline, painstakingly detailing their last weeks, even months, of life. It was a process that demanded patience, a willingness to sift through mundane appointments, routine interactions, and seemingly insignificant events, searching for the anomaly, the flicker of disruption that might betray a hidden narrative.

With Elias Thorne, she mapped out his days with the precision of a clockmaker. His solitary walks in the park, his regular visits to the antique market, his infrequent phone calls with a distant relative – each entry was a meticulously placed cog in the machinery of his routine. But as she delved deeper, into the weeks preceding his death, a subtle shift began to emerge. There were entries marked "unexplained distress," moments where Thorne's usual calm demeanor had reportedly wavered. A neighbor recalled seeing him arguing with a stranger outside his apartment building, a heated exchange that ended with Thorne visibly shaken. A shopkeeper at his favorite bookstore mentioned Thorne purchasing a collection of obscure poetry, an unusual purchase for a man known for his practical interests. These were not smoking guns, but they were whispers, faint but distinct, of a man whose carefully constructed world was beginning to fray.

She did the same for Clara Bellweather. The opera singer's life was a whirlwind of rehearsals, performances, and social engagements. Yet, Gwen focused on the quieter moments, the periods of solitude between the applause. Clara had been seen visiting a therapist, her sessions initially described as routine stress management, but later hinting at deeper anxieties. There were records of late-night phone calls to an unknown number, conversations that her agent claimed to know nothing about. A trusted dresser mentioned Clara's increasing paranoia, her habit of checking and rechecking the locks on her dressing room door, her insistence that she was being watched. Gwen meticulously documented each instance, each fleeting shadow of unease, building a mosaic of a woman grappling with unseen forces.

The process was grueling. Hours bled into days, fueled by lukewarm coffee and the quiet determination that kept Gwen tethered to her desk. She found herself losing track of time, the world outside her office fading into an irrelevant hum. The faces of the victims began to blur, their stories intertwining in her mind, each narrative a variation on a theme of fear and isolation. She remembered the initial reports, the pronouncements of a lone, deranged killer, but her gut screamed otherwise. There was a deliberate hand at play, a meticulous planner orchestrating these tragedies with a chilling precision.

Gwen shifted her attention to a third file, that of a young architect named Daniel Hayes, found dead in his minimalist apartment, the scene eerily clean, almost sterile. Hayes was the antithesis of Thorne and Bellweather – young, ambitious, and seemingly well-connected. Yet, as Gwen painstakingly reconstructed his final days, a familiar pattern began to emerge. Hayes had recently withdrawn a significant sum of money from his savings, the purpose of which remained unclear. He had also been seen attending a series of late-night, clandestine meetings in dimly lit bars, his companions a shifting group of individuals with shadowy reputations. His colleagues spoke of a growing restlessness, a sense of being on the verge of a major breakthrough, but also of an overwhelming pressure, a feeling that he was being pushed to his limits.

The common denominator was not a shared profession or social circle. It was a shared experience of mounting pressure, of a life veering off its predictable course, of encountering something – or someone – that disrupted the established order. Gwen sketched out a diagram on her notepad, connecting the three victims with faint lines. Thorne, the recluse whose quiet life was shattered by a violent intrusion. Bellweather, the star whose public life masked a private torment. Hayes, the rising star whose ambition led him into dangerous territories. What could possibly link such disparate lives?

She considered the nature of their deaths. Each was brutal, yet meticulously staged, almost theatrical in their presentation. It spoke of a killer with a profound understanding of human psychology, someone who knew how to exploit vulnerabilities, how to sow seeds of doubt and fear. This wasn't random violence; it was targeted, personal, and deeply unsettling.

Gwen leaned closer to the Thorne file. The antique clock. It had been stopped at precisely 3:17 AM. A meaningless detail to most, but to Gwen, it was a deliberate act, a signature. She cross-referenced this with the Bellweather case. The opera singer's music box, found open on her vanity, was also frozen, its delicate melody silenced at a specific point. And in Hayes' apartment, a blueprint for a new skyscraper lay on his desk, a single line of code etched into the margin, a fragment of a larger program. Each victim, a silent testament to the killer's obsession with time, with precision, with control.

The killer was not just taking lives; they were manipulating the narrative, leaving behind cryptic clues that spoke of a grand, disturbing design. Gwen felt a shiver trace its way down her spine. This was no ordinary spree. This was a performance, and the victims were merely actors in a play orchestrated by a madman. She began to meticulously record the time of death for each victim, searching for a chronological progression, a pattern in the timing itself. Thorne: 3:17 AM. Bellweather: 11:42 PM. Hayes: 6:01 AM. No obvious correlation. But perhaps the timing wasn't about the specific hour, but about the *interval* between the events. She calculated the days between each murder, then the hours. The numbers swam before her eyes, a chaotic jumble. She needed a different approach.

She started to focus on the “unexplained distress” in each victim’s timeline. For Thorne, it was the argument with the stranger. For Bellweather, it was the paranoia. For Hayes, it was the pressure and the clandestine meetings. These weren’t isolated incidents; they were periods where the victims seemed to be aware of a looming threat, a sense that something was irrevocably wrong. Gwen began to hypothesize that these periods of distress were not merely psychological, but were directly linked to the killer’s actions, their subtle manipulation of the victims’ lives. The killer was not just waiting for the right moment; they were actively creating it, engineering the circumstances that would lead to their victims' downfall.

She recalled a detail from Clara Bellweather’s final days. The singer had been rehearsing a new aria, a tragic piece about a woman trapped in a gilded cage, consumed by a love that was slowly destroying her. Clara had reportedly been unusually affected by the music, her performance taking on a raw, visceral intensity. The composer, a notoriously eccentric figure, had apparently gifted Clara a unique, handcrafted music box shortly before her death. Gwen retrieved the composer’s file. He was a man known for his psychological dramas, his ability to tap into the darkest corners of the human psyche. Had he somehow been involved? Or was this a mere coincidence, a red herring in a carefully constructed labyrinth?

Gwen’s gaze returned to Daniel Hayes. The blueprint. The single line of code. She had initially dismissed it as a technical detail, a stray mark on an otherwise pristine document. But what if it wasn’t random? What if it was a message, a fragment of a larger, encrypted communication? She contacted a forensic computer analyst, a wizened old hacker named “Zero” who operated out of a dimly lit basement filled with blinking servers. Zero, after hours of intense work, confirmed Gwen’s suspicions. The line of code was not a fragment of a program, but a key, a password. A password to what, however, remained a mystery.

The puzzle pieces were beginning to coalesce, forming a fragmented image of a highly intelligent, deeply disturbed individual. This wasn't just about murder; it was about control, about the meticulous manipulation of lives and narratives. Gwen felt a growing sense of urgency. The killer was not just a predator; they were an artist, and their canvas was the human psyche. Each victim represented a masterpiece of terror, a testament to their ability to orchestrate destruction with surgical precision. She looked at the timelines spread before her, the meticulously documented periods of distress, the cryptic clues left behind. The investigator's net was tightening, not with brute force, but with the intricate, invisible threads of logic and observation, slowly but surely closing in on the elusive killer. The silence of her office was broken only by the soft clicking of her pen against the notepad, each stroke a step closer to revealing the truth.

The hours blurred into a single, relentless pursuit. Gwen felt as though she were navigating a labyrinth constructed from the fragmented lives of the deceased. Elias Thorne, the horologist; Clara Bellweather, the opera diva; Daniel Hayes, the ambitious architect. Each a distinct melody, yet she sensed a discordant harmony binding them together. Her initial approach, the meticulous charting of timelines and the careful dissection of their final days, had revealed a chilling consistency: the calculated disruption of routine, the subtle introduction of chaos that preceded the ultimate, violent conclusion. But the 'how' was becoming clearer than the 'why,' and the perpetrator's methods suggested a mind that was not merely impulsive, but deliberate, almost academic in its execution.

She pushed aside the disparate case files, her attention now drawn to the periphery, to the peripheral details that had seemed insignificant at first glance. The peculiar placement of Thorne's antique clock, its hands frozen at 3:17 AM. The precisely timed silence of Clara's music box. The solitary, cryptic line of code etched into Hayes' blueprint. These weren't just symbolic gestures; they felt like annotations, like markers left by a craftsman proud of his work. A cold dread began to coalesce in the pit of her stomach. What if these weren't random acts of artistic expression, but rather… instructions?

Gwen's gaze drifted to a dusty shelf in her office, filled with tomes on criminology, psychology, and sociology. She'd always been a voracious reader, her mind a sponge for information that might illuminate the darkest corners of human behavior. Her fingers brushed against a worn spine, a book she hadn't opened in years: "The Architect of Aberrations: A Study of Serial Perpetrators and Their Methodologies" by Dr. Alistair Finch. Finch was a controversial figure in forensic psychology, his theories often dismissed as too esoteric, too speculative. But Gwen had always found a strange resonance in his writings, a disturbing insight into the minds of those who operated outside the bounds of conventional morality.

She pulled the book from the shelf, its pages brittle with age. Finch posited that highly intelligent serial offenders, particularly those with a narcissistic or obsessive-compulsive disorder, often developed complex, ritualistic methodologies. They didn't just kill; they enacted a script, a performance designed to satisfy a deeply ingrained psychological need. He spoke of "signature acts" not as mere calling cards, but as integral components of a carefully constructed process. And then, he introduced a concept that sent a jolt through Gwen: the idea of a 'manual' or 'guidebook.'

Finch theorized that such perpetrators, driven by a need for perfection and control, would often meticulously document their methods. Not just for their own reference, but as a testament to their perceived superiority, a blueprint for their twisted art. These manuals, he suggested, were often kept in coded formats, disguised as personal journals or technical documents, containing detailed instructions on everything from victim selection and psychological manipulation to the precise staging of the crime scene and the timing of their 'grand finale.' The goal was not just to commit murder, but to achieve a state of perfect execution, a flawless performance that validated their warped worldview.

Gwen's heart began to pound in her chest. She reread the passages on Finch's 'manual' theory, her eyes scanning the dense academic prose. He described how these individuals often drew inspiration from existing ideologies, philosophical concepts, or even technical disciplines. They would then adapt and innovate, creating their own unique 'operating system' for murder. The timing, the staging, the symbolic elements – they weren't random; they were the carefully chosen parameters of their self-published handbook.

Could this explain the precision, the almost theatrical nature of Thorne's, Bellweather's, and Hayes' deaths? The seemingly symbolic timing of the clocks and music boxes? The cryptic code on the blueprint? Gwen felt a surge of adrenaline, a sense of clarity cutting through the fog of confusion. This wasn't just a string of isolated murders; it was a systematic operation, guided by a chillingly consistent doctrine.

She began to connect the dots with renewed fervor. Thorne, the horologist, obsessed with time. Bellweather, the opera singer, her life a dramatic performance. Hayes, the architect, a builder of structures, both physical and abstract. Each victim seemed to represent a different facet of the perpetrator's obsession, a living embodiment of the principles outlined in their dark manual. Thorne embodied the concept of time itself, its relentless march and its potential for precise manipulation. Bellweather represented the performance, the carefully curated illusion that masked underlying turmoil. Hayes, the architect, symbolized the structural integrity, the meticulous planning and execution required to build – or destroy.

Gwen's mind raced, recalling obscure news reports and unsolved cases she'd encountered over the years. Were there others? Had there been other victims, perhaps less publicized, who fit this pattern? She began to scour online databases, historical crime archives, and even academic journals, searching for any mention of meticulously staged murders, of unusual timing, of symbolic elements that seemed to defy rational explanation. She was looking for echoes, for whispers of this 'manual' operating in the past.

Her search led her to a series of unsolved disappearances from a decade prior, clustered in different cities, involving individuals from seemingly disparate walks of life. A renowned mathematician who vanished without a trace, leaving behind a complex equation scribbled on a whiteboard that no one could decipher. A celebrated choreographer who was found dead in her studio, surrounded by an intricate pattern of ropes and silks, her body positioned in a pose that seemed to defy gravity. A renowned cartographer who was discovered in his meticulously organized office, a single, unfinished map spread across his desk, depicting a territory that didn't exist. The details were sparse, the connections tenuous, but Gwen felt a prickle of recognition. The underlying theme of precision, of symbolic representation, of a methodical approach to death, was undeniable.

She cross-referenced the dates and locations of these older cases with Thorne's, Bellweather's, and Hayes'. A faint geographical pattern began to emerge, a subtle clustering of events that suggested a perpetrator who moved with purpose, perhaps following a predetermined route or targeting specific types of individuals in a particular order. It was like watching a spider meticulously weave its web, each strand intentionally placed, leading to a central point of capture.

Gwen felt a growing sense of urgency. The 'manual' theory wasn't just a hypothesis anymore; it was a terrifyingly plausible explanation. This killer was not just a murderer; they were a meticulous planner, a craftsman of death, who viewed their crimes as a form of instruction, a demonstration of their perceived mastery over life and its ultimate cessation. They were not just killing; they were teaching, albeit through the most horrific means imaginable.

She imagined the manual itself. Was it a physical book? A digital file? Encrypted? The line of code from Hayes' blueprint now seemed incredibly significant. It was a key, as Zero had confirmed, but a key to what? A hidden file? A secure server? A digital vault of the killer's sick philosophy? The perpetrator was clearly intelligent, technologically savvy, and deeply invested in the secrecy and preservation of their methodology.

Gwen delved deeper into Finch's work, focusing on the psychological profile of perpetrators who create such manuals. Finch described them as often possessing an inflated sense of intellect, a deep-seated need for control, and a profound lack of empathy. They viewed themselves as superior beings, their actions justified by their own internal logic. They craved recognition, not in a conventional sense, but as masters of their craft, as those who understood the fundamental truths of existence that others were too ignorant or too weak to grasp.

This explained the staged scenes, the symbolic timing, the calculated omissions. Each element was a carefully crafted lesson, a demonstration of the perpetrator's intellect and their control over their victims' fates. Thorne's death was a lesson in the malleability of time. Bellweather's was a lesson in the fragility of perceived perfection. Hayes' was a lesson in the inevitable collapse of ambition when faced with insurmountable forces. The killer was leaving breadcrumbs, not for law enforcement to follow, but for a select few, or perhaps for posterity, to understand their grand design.

Gwen felt a cold, hard knot tighten in her stomach. She was no longer just investigating a series of murders; she was trying to decipher a twisted manifesto, a dark education delivered through bloodshed. The perpetrator was not just a killer; they were a teacher, and their classroom was the scene of the crime. The 'manual' was their textbook, and the victims were their unfortunate students, their lives sacrificed to impart a chilling, final lesson. The investigator's net, once a tool for ensnaring a simple murderer, now felt like an instrument for unraveling a complex, horrifying curriculum. The silence in her office seemed to amplify the imagined rustle of pages, the unspoken words of a killer's chilling guide. The tightening net was not just closing in on a killer; it was closing in on an ideology, a philosophy of destruction meticulously documented and brutally enacted.

The air in the precinct was thick with the usual pre-dawn chill, a subtle but persistent reminder of the long hours and the gnawing anxieties that clung to every detective.

Gwen, however, felt a different kind of cold radiating from the fluorescent lights overhead. It was the cold of indifference, of institutional inertia, a stark contrast to the burning urgency that fueled her own pursuit. She'd spent the night poring over Dr. Finch's 'The Architect of Aberrations,' her desk a chaotic landscape of open files, highlighted passages, and half-empty coffee cups. The 'manual' theory had taken root, a terrifyingly logical explanation for the meticulous, almost ritualistic nature of the recent murders. Thorne, Bellweather, Hayes – they weren't random victims; they were pedagogical sacrifices in the killer's twisted curriculum.

She'd tried to broach the subject with her colleagues, hinting at a deeper pattern, a disturbing methodology. The reactions ranged from polite nods to outright skepticism. Detective Miller, a man whose career was built on a foundation of by-the-book procedure, had merely grunted, "Gwen, you're chasing ghosts. Thorne was a robbery gone wrong, Clara a jealous lover, Hayes an industrial accident. We've closed those files." The dismissiveness stung, a familiar ache that echoed the isolation she'd felt after her brother's unsolved case. It wasn't just that they didn't believe her; it was that they seemed unwilling to even consider the possibility.

This morning, however, the resistance had coalesced into a more formidable, institutional force: Chief Vance. He'd summoned her to his office, the Spartan space a reflection of his no-nonsense, results-oriented leadership. The framed commendations on the wall seemed to mock her own perceived lack of progress. Vance, a man whose face was a roadmap of precinct politics and tough decisions, leaned back in his chair, his expression unreadable.

"Gwen," he began, his voice a low rumble, devoid of any warmth, "I've been reviewing your recent activity logs. You're spending an inordinate amount of time on cold cases, on tangential research. Frankly, it's becoming a distraction."

Gwen took a steadying breath. "Chief, I believe the recent deaths of Elias Thorne, Clara Bellweather, and Daniel Hayes are not isolated incidents. There's a pattern, a deliberate methodology that suggests a single perpetrator."

Vance steepled his fingers, his gaze fixed on her. "A pattern? Or are you seeing patterns because you *want* to see them? Your brother's case... it's been a heavy burden, Gwen. We all understand that. But we can't let personal grief cloud our professional judgment. Miller's teams have investigated those cases thoroughly. There's nothing connecting them."

The mention of her brother, a ghost that still haunted the edges of her life, was a low blow. It was the weapon of choice for those who couldn't counter an argument on its merits: attack the arguer's emotional state. "With all due respect, Chief, my brother's case is why I'm so attuned to these details. And these aren't just 'details.' The timing, the staging, the symbolic elements... they're too precise to be coincidence. I've uncovered a theory, a possibility, that these murders are part of a larger narrative, a carefully constructed plan."

Vance's lips thinned. "A narrative? Gwen, this isn't a novel you're writing. This is a police investigation. We deal with facts, with evidence, not with... theories about perpetrators' 'narratives.' What kind of evidence do you have to support this elaborate fiction?"

"I've been researching the work of Dr. Alistair Finch," Gwen began, her voice gaining a determined edge. "He theorized about serial offenders who create what he called 'manuals' – meticulously documented guides for their crimes. The precision in these deaths, the almost artistic presentation... it aligns perfectly with Finch's profile."

Vance let out a short, sharp laugh, a sound that grated on Gwen's nerves. "Finch? The man's theories are considered fringe, Gwen. Academia barely tolerates him, and you're basing your investigation on his work? You're grasping at straws. The operative word here is 'straws.' These are unrelated incidents, and you're wasting valuable resources chasing phantoms." He leaned forward, his tone hardening. "I need you focused on active cases. I need you following leads that lead to arrests, not delving into psychological profiles from discredited academics. We have a robbery-homicide, a domestic dispute, and a workplace accident. Those are the facts. The rest is... noise."

The word 'noise' hung in the air, a dismissal of her insights, her dedication, her growing conviction. Gwen felt a familiar wave of frustration wash over her, but she pushed it down, refusing to let it derail her. "Chief, the code found on Daniel Hayes' blueprint, the one Zero confirmed is a decryption key, it's not random. It's part of this... this manual. It's a directive, a component of the perpetrator's system. If we dismiss it as noise, we're ignoring a crucial piece of the puzzle."

"Zero is a civilian consultant, Gwen, and frankly, his involvement is on the edge of what I'm comfortable with. And a decryption key for what? A disgruntled employee's manifesto? A gamer's cheat code? We've had tech teams look at it. It leads nowhere. It's an anomaly, nothing more." Vance stood up, signaling the end of the conversation. "I want you back on the streets, working with your assigned units. I want tangible progress on cases that matter. If you can't do that, Gwen, then we'll have to have a more serious conversation about your future here."

The threat, veiled but potent, hung heavy in the air. Gwen knew Vance wasn't trying to punish her out of spite, but out of a perceived need to maintain order, to manage resources efficiently, and perhaps, to protect himself from the embarrassment of a high-profile investigation going off the rails. He saw her intensity as a liability, her theories as a dangerous deviation from established protocol. Her dedication, which she believed was bringing her closer to the truth, was being interpreted as stubbornness, as an inability to let go of a personal crusade.

Leaving Vance's office, Gwen felt a profound sense of isolation. It wasn't just the weight of the unsolved murders; it was the weight of disbelief, of professional censure. The hallways of the precinct, once a symbol of shared purpose and collective effort, now felt like a labyrinth of unspoken doubts and political maneuvering. Each corner turned, each familiar face encountered, seemed to carry an unspoken judgment. Some officers averted their gaze, others offered curt nods that felt more like pity than camaraderie. They'd heard the whispers, seen Vance's displeasure. Gwen was becoming an outlier, a detective whose increasingly unorthodox methods were a source of concern rather than admiration.

She found herself walking through the bullpen, the hum of activity a stark contrast to the silence in her own mind. Miller glanced up from his desk, a smug half-smile playing on his lips. "Heard the Chief gave you a talking-to, Gwen. Guess the ghost hunting's over, huh?"

Gwen ignored him, her gaze fixed on the framed evidence board, a mosaic of crimes and culprits, each a story in itself. But her story, the one she was trying to write, felt like it was being actively erased by the very institution meant to support it. The political currents within the precinct ran deeper than she'd initially realized, and her relentless pursuit of the truth was beginning to make her a political target. Chief Vance, a master of navigating these currents, saw her as a potential liability, a rogue element that threatened the perceived order and efficiency of his command. Her obsession, the very thing that drove her to uncover the horrifying truth, was being framed as a symptom of her own psychological instability, a projection of her grief onto a canvas of unsolved crimes.

She thought of the 'manual' again, the hypothetical blueprint of a killer's mind. It was a meticulously crafted document, designed for a specific purpose, intended to be understood by a select audience. And in a strange, twisted way, she felt as though the precinct itself had become a microcosm of that same dynamic. There was a recognized narrative, an accepted order of operations, and anything that deviated from it was dismissed as 'noise.' Her attempts to introduce the concept of the manual, to explain the perpetrator's meticulous planning and symbolic intent, were met with the same resistance as a poorly formatted report or a misplaced piece of evidence.

The obstacles in her way weren't just the physical distances between crime scenes or the elusiveness of a suspect. They were the bureaucratic hurdles, the ingrained skepticism, the fear of the unknown that permeated the very fabric of the department. Vance's words echoed in her mind: "We deal with facts, with evidence, not with... theories." But what if the 'facts' themselves were carefully constructed lies, designed to obscure a deeper, more disturbing truth? What if the 'evidence' was a carefully curated tableau, meant to mislead and misdirect?

She returned to her desk, the cold dread intensifying. The 'manual' theory was her only viable path forward, her only way to make sense of the fragmented pieces. But pursuing it meant swimming against a powerful tide. It meant navigating a treacherous landscape of office politics, where her dedication could be misconstrued as obsession, her insights as delusion. The tightening net wasn't just the killer's approach; it was the increasingly suffocating embrace of her own colleagues, their disbelief forming a cage around her investigation. She was a detective on the outside, looking in, trying to convince a closed system that a monster was operating within its very walls, leaving behind not just corpses, but chilling lessons. The weight of it all pressed down on her, a tangible force in the quiet hum of the precinct, a testament to the isolation that often accompanied the pursuit of truth in the darkest of places. The challenge wasn't just catching a killer; it was surviving the bureaucracy that stood between her and justice.

The precinct, usually a cacophony of ringing phones and hurried footsteps, had fallen into a sort of weary quiet. The pre-dawn air, though stale and tinged with the metallic scent of old coffee, felt charged with an unvoiced tension. Gwen sat hunched over her desk, the lukewarm dregs of her coffee mirroring the cooling embers of her initial hope. Chief Vance's dismissal had been more than just a reprimand; it had been an act of institutional censorship, a deliberate attempt to steer her away from the path she knew was the right one. The word 'noise' still echoed in her mind, a dismissive wave of Vance's hand that had effectively silenced her concerns, labeling them as the ramblings of a grief-stricken detective.

She ran a hand over the worn cover of Dr. Alistair Finch's 'The Architect of Aberrations.' The book was her sanctuary and her torment, a chilling validation of her deepest fears. Finch's theories, dismissed by Vance as fringe, spoke of perpetrators who didn't just kill; they educated, they manipulated, they orchestrated elaborate psychological dramas. Thorne, Bellweather, Hayes – their deaths, so disparate on the surface, now seemed to form a terrifying syllogism in Gwen's mind. Each a lesson, each a building block in a larger, monstrous architecture of aberrant behavior.

The 'manual' theory wasn't just a working hypothesis anymore; it was a chillingly coherent narrative that explained the meticulous staging, the symbolic resonance of the victims' professions, and the chillingly precise methods of their demise. Thorne, the financial advisor, a symbol of greed and systemic corruption. Bellweather, the historian, a guardian of narratives, silenced to perhaps rewrite history. Hayes, the architect, his plans twisted into a macabre blueprint for death. They were chapters in a book being written in blood, each death a carefully chosen illustration of a twisted lesson.

She remembered the detail about Hayes' blueprints, the faint, almost imperceptible annotation that Zero, her civilian consultant, had identified as a decryption key. Vance had dismissed it as an anomaly, a digital dead end. But Gwen felt a prickle of intuition, a stubborn refusal to let that detail be relegated to the realm of 'noise.' Zero had been adamant. "It's not just random code, Gwen," he'd insisted via a secure line earlier, his voice a low, urgent murmur. "The structure, the sequencing... it's an instruction set. Like a key to a locked file, or a sequence to activate a program." He'd been working on it relentlessly, sifting through reams of code, his usual sardonic wit replaced by a grim focus.

The precinct hummed around her, a hive of activity that felt increasingly alien. Detectives bustled past, their conversations a blur of case files and suspect profiles that felt frustratingly mundane compared to the existential horror that gripped her. Detective Miller, a man who embodied the precinct's rigid adherence to procedure, caught her eye as he strode past, his gaze holding a mixture of pity and a thinly veiled disdain. He'd been one of the first to dismiss her theories, his pragmatic mind unwilling to entertain anything that deviated from his well-worn playbook. "Still chasing shadows, Gwen?" he'd asked earlier, his tone dripping with mock sympathy. "Vance is right. Focus on what's real, what's tangible."

Tangible. The word felt like a taunt. What was more tangible than the undeniable patterns she was uncovering, the chilling echoes between the victims and the meticulous, almost artistic, presentation of their deaths? She'd spent hours meticulously cross-referencing information, looking for any crack in the façade of randomness Vance and Miller so readily accepted. It was in these late hours, fueled by stale coffee and a gnawing dread, that the faintest glimmers of confirmation began to emerge, not from official channels, but from the periphery, from the shadows of the established narrative.

Her focus sharpened on a small, seemingly insignificant detail from Clara Bellweather's case. Bellweather, the historian, had been found in her meticulously organized study, surrounded by antique books and historical artifacts. The official report had classified the scene as undisturbed, a testament to the killer's efficiency. But Gwen had re-examined the crime scene photographs, zooming in on the periphery, on the details that might have been overlooked in the rush to label it a straightforward homicide. She'd noticed it then, a faint indentation on the spine of a thick, leather-bound volume on her desk, almost obscured by the shadow cast by a nearby lamp. It looked like the imprint of a small, metallic object, something that had been pressed firmly against the book for an extended period.

It was a tenuous lead, easily explained away. A dropped pen, a misplaced artifact. But coupled with Finch's descriptions of 'instructional trauma,' of perpetrators who used objects and environments as teaching tools, it began to coalesce into something more sinister. Finch had detailed how some offenders would leave subtle clues, embedded within the victim's environment, to mark their 'students' progress or to communicate specific messages to themselves or a hidden audience. This imprint, so small and easily missed, felt like a deliberate mark.

She'd contacted Clara Bellweather's sister, Eleanor, a quiet woman who was still reeling from the shock of her sister's death. Eleanor, though distraught, had been cooperative, providing Gwen with access to Clara's personal effects. It was in Clara's desk, beneath a stack of meticulously organized research papers, that Gwen found it – a small, tarnished silver locket, intricately engraved with a floral pattern. It was identical in size and shape to the impression on the book's spine. Eleanor confirmed it had belonged to their grandmother, a treasured heirloom Clara always wore. The locket was missing.

"Clara never took it off," Eleanor had said, her voice trembling. "She said it was her anchor, a reminder of where she came from. She was very... particular about it. If she took it off, it would be for a very good reason, or it would be because someone forced her to."

The implication sent a cold shiver down Gwen's spine. The killer hadn't just taken the locket; they had used it. They had pressed it against the book, leaving an imprint, a subtle but deliberate mark. It was a detail that no one else had considered, a detail that fit Finch's model of symbolic communication. The killer wasn't just leaving a signature; they were leaving a message, a deliberate instruction embedded within the crime scene itself. It was a confirmation of the 'manual' theory, a tangible piece of evidence that spoke volumes about the perpetrator's meticulous planning and psychological manipulation.

But with this glimmer of validation came a profound and suffocating dread. The precision of the act, the deliberate nature of the imprint, underscored the killer's intelligence and their chilling dedication to their twisted methodology. This wasn't the work of a frenzied killer; it was the calculated move of a master strategist, someone who understood the power of symbols and the psychological impact of subtle manipulation. The locket, once a symbol of familial connection, had been co-opted, transformed into an instrument of terror, a tool in the killer's macabre curriculum.

Gwen stared at the crime scene photo, the faint indentation now screaming at her. It was a mark of genius, of a mind operating on a level that transcended conventional criminal behavior. It was a testament to the fact that the killer was not only intelligent but deeply disturbed, capable of orchestrating these events with a chilling level of premeditation. The 'manual' wasn't just a theoretical concept; it was a tangible, evolving document, and the locket imprint was a new entry, a coded lesson designed to be deciphered by those who understood the killer's language.

She remembered another detail, this one from Elias Thorne's case. Thorne, the financial advisor, had been found in his high-rise office, slumped over his desk. The cause of death had been a single, precise stab wound to the heart. The weapon had never been recovered. But Gwen recalled a peculiar detail from the initial sweep: a small, intricately folded origami crane, made from a piece of what appeared to be high-quality bond paper, tucked neatly into Thorne's breast pocket. The crime scene techs had initially dismissed it as a random piece of debris, perhaps dropped by Thorne himself. But the precision of the fold, the almost impossible neatness of it, had nagged at her.

Now, with the locket imprint fresh in her mind, the origami crane took on a new, terrifying significance. Finch's writings extensively detailed the use of symbolic objects in ritualistic killings. Origami, with its inherent complexity and meditative qualities, was often cited as a practice associated with order, patience, and intricate design. Could the crane be another coded message, another lesson from the 'manual'?

She requested Thorne's personal effects from the evidence locker. Among the standard items – wallet, keys, watch – she found a small, nondescript notebook. It was filled with financial notations, market analyses, and the usual jargon of the trading world. However, tucked away in the back, almost an afterthought, was a series of meticulously drawn diagrams. They weren't financial charts. They were complex, geometric patterns, almost like blueprints for intricate constructions. And at the bottom of one page, a single, elegantly folded origami crane, identical in style to the one found at the crime scene.

A cold dread, sharper and more potent than anything she had felt before, washed over her. Thorne hadn't just been a victim; he had been a student, perhaps even a practitioner, of the killer's disturbing methodology. The diagrams in his notebook were not his own; they were clues, instructions, illustrations from the very 'manual' she was trying to decipher. The killer was not just leaving messages; they were leaving exercises, assignments, designed to reinforce specific lessons or to test the skills of their chosen audience.

Gwen leaned back in her chair, the fluorescent lights of the precinct casting long, distorted shadows across her desk. The small, silver locket and the origami crane, once disparate, disconnected anomalies, now formed a terrifying nexus. They were tangible proof, concrete evidence that her 'noise' was, in fact, the very signal she had been searching for. The killer was intelligent, methodical, and deeply invested in their own warped pedagogy. And they were escalating.

The realization brought no comfort, only a heightened sense of urgency and a chilling premonition of what was to come. The 'manual' wasn't just a theoretical construct; it was a living, breathing entity, a deadly curriculum being implemented with chilling precision. The tightening net wasn't just a metaphor for the killer's approach; it was the very real and suffocating embrace of an investigation that was being systematically undermined from within. Chief Vance and his dismissal of her theories felt less like bureaucratic obstruction and more like a deliberate blindfold, designed to prevent anyone from seeing the monster operating in plain sight. The pieces were falling into place, but the picture they formed was one of escalating danger, of a predator who was not just killing, but teaching, and the lessons were deadly. The investigation had taken a terrifying turn, moving from the realm of mere homicide to that of a meticulously planned, psychologically driven campaign. Gwen knew, with a certainty that chilled her to the bone, that this was only the beginning.

The city, a sprawling organism of concrete and flickering neon, pulsed with a rhythm that was both indifferent and hypnotic. From his vantage point, a meticulously chosen perch overlooking the city's arteries, Adam felt its thrum as if it were his own. The pre-dawn chill did little to dampen the warmth that bloomed in his chest – the satisfaction of a game well played, and the tantalizing anticipation of the next move. He watched the distant headlights trace ephemeral patterns on the asphalt, each one a potential player, a potential pawn. Gwen's efforts, the frantic scurrying of a trapped insect, were a distant hum, a minor inconvenience rather than a true threat. She was so focused on the threads of the past, on the fallen pieces of his carefully constructed puzzle, that she failed to see the new game board being laid out before her.

He traced the rim of his coffee cup, the ceramic cool against his fingertips. The lukewarm liquid was a far cry from the boiling urgency Gwen undoubtedly felt, drowning in her stale coffee and the suffocating weight of institutional doubt. She saw patterns, yes. She was learning. But she was learning the wrong lessons, or rather, she was learning the lessons he *wanted* her to learn. The locket, the crane – they were meticulously placed breadcrumbs, designed to lead her down a specific, carefully manicured path. Each piece of evidence was a testament to his mastery, a demonstration of his ability to weave a narrative that resonated with her burgeoning understanding of his work, yet simultaneously steered her away from the true heart of his operation.

His gaze drifted, settling on a particular cluster of buildings several blocks away. A sleek, modern structure, all glass and polished chrome, housing a prestigious art gallery. The current exhibition featured a collection of abstract sculptures, bold, challenging pieces that spoke of disruption and transformation. It was a fitting backdrop, he mused, for the next act. The artist, a reclusive figure named Julian Vance – no relation to the Chief, a fact that amused him – was known for his provocative work, for pushing the boundaries of perception. Vance was a craftsman, an artisan of form and void, and he was about to become the centerpiece of Adam's next lesson.

Adam had been observing Vance for weeks. Not with the overt surveillance of a detective, but with the patient, almost artistic observation of a collector. He knew Vance's routines: the late nights spent in his studio, the solitary walks through the city's quieter districts, the almost ritualistic way he interacted with his art. Vance was a man driven by a singular vision, a relentless pursuit of perfection that mirrored Adam's own in many ways. He was, in essence, a kindred spirit, albeit one who channelled his creative energies into a far less... impactful medium.

The official narrative Gwen was chasing was a complex tapestry of symbolic murder, a perpetrator who educated through execution. It was a narrative that required careful curation, and Adam was its meticulous editor. The previous victims had served their purpose, each death a carefully articulated chapter designed to impart specific, if painful, knowledge. Thorne, the architect of financial systems, had demonstrated the fragility of perceived order. Bellweather, the guardian of historical narratives, had shown the malleability of truth. Hayes, the very builder of the physical world, had illustrated the inherent potential for destruction within creation. These were foundational lessons, designed to prepare the observer for a deeper understanding.

But Gwen was still stuck in the prologue, poring over the footnotes and the elaborate illustrations. She was so preoccupied with the *how* that she was missing the *why*. The locket and the crane, while significant pieces of his carefully constructed narrative, were merely supplementary materials. They were the historical context, the footnotes in a larger, more profound work. Vance's exhibition, on the other hand, was about to become the climax, the pivotal demonstration of a more complex, more dangerous concept.

He recalled a recent visit to the gallery, a few days prior. He'd moved through the hushed space with a practiced anonymity, blending into the small crowd of art patrons and critics. He'd observed Vance, a wiry figure with sharp, intelligent eyes, engaging in a quiet conversation with a gallery owner. Vance's hands, stained with paint and clay, moved with an elegant precision as he gestured towards a towering, angular sculpture crafted from reclaimed steel. Adam had felt a surge of something akin to admiration. Vance understood form, he understood the interplay of light and shadow, the way an object could command space and evoke emotion.

Adam had circled the sculpture, his mind already weaving connections. The sharp edges, the deliberate asymmetry, the stark contrast between the raw, industrial materials and the refined artistic intent. It was a piece that spoke of conflict, of forces colliding. He'd felt the faint vibration of the city beneath his feet, the distant rumble of traffic a counterpoint to the silent tension emanating from the artwork. Vance, in his own way, was already exploring the very themes Adam sought to dissect.

He remembered overhearing a snippet of conversation between Vance and a patron. "It's about the spaces between things, you see," Vance had explained, his voice low and earnest. "The negative space. It's often more telling than the object itself. It defines the object, gives it context, gives it meaning."

The words resonated deeply within Adam. The spaces between. The unseen connections. The implied meanings. Gwen was so focused on the tangible objects, the locket, the crane, the method of death, that she was ignoring the vast, critical expanse of the negative space. That was where the true lessons lay. That was where the real manipulation occurred.

He pictured Vance's studio, a chaotic yet organized haven of creativity. Canvases leaned against walls, splattered with vibrant hues. Tools lay scattered across workbenches, each bearing the marks of its use. In the center of the room, bathed in the cool light filtering through a large skylight, sat Vance's latest work-in-progress. It was a sculpture of a different nature, more organic, more fluid than those on display at the gallery. It was a piece that, in its nascent form, hinted at vulnerability, at a raw, exposed core.

Adam had acquired a small, almost insignificant piece of Vance's personal life, something so innocuous that its retrieval had been effortlessly simple. A discarded sketchbook, left carelessly near a public park bin. Inside, among the charcoal sketches and watercolor studies, was a series of preliminary drawings for the new sculpture. They depicted not just the form, but the intricate internal structure, the hidden framework that would ultimately support the more visible, outward shell. It was a glimpse into the artist's process, a peek behind the curtain of creation.

He had spent hours studying those drawings, not for their artistic merit, but for their underlying message. They spoke of a duality, of a carefully constructed exterior masking a complex, perhaps even fragile, interior. It was a metaphor for the very nature of the human psyche, a concept that had fascinated Adam for years. Vance, by pouring his understanding of this duality into his art, had inadvertently created the perfect canvas for Adam's next demonstration.

The next move had to be subtle, almost imperceptible. Gwen was looking for overt signs, for the bloody handprint on the wall. Adam specialized in the whisper, the suggestion, the quiet alteration of perception. He needed to create a scenario that would resonate with Vance's artistic sensibilities, a situation that would amplify the themes already present in his work, and in doing so, create a powerful, undeniable lesson for anyone capable of truly seeing.

He envisioned Vance, alone in his studio, surrounded by the tools of his trade. The air thick with the scent of turpentine and oil paint. The silence broken only by the gentle scratching of charcoal on paper, or the soft thud of a hammer against metal. Vance, so dedicated to his craft, so immersed in his own world of form and meaning. He would be so focused on the external, on the creation of beauty and impact, that he would be blind to the subtle intrusion, the almost imperceptible shift in his environment.

Adam knew that Vance, like his previous victims, possessed a certain hubris, a belief in his own control and understanding of his world. It was this belief, this inherent confidence in his own vision, that made him such a perfect candidate. He wouldn't expect to be a subject, only an observer, or perhaps an unwitting contributor to a grander design.

He considered the details of the upcoming exhibition. The opening night reception. The throngs of people, the clinking glasses, the murmur of conversation. It was a stage set for performance, for revelation. Vance would be there, basking in the admiration, his work speaking for him. But Adam intended to add his own voice to the chorus, a voice that would speak of a different kind of truth, a truth that lay not in the sculpted form, but in the empty spaces around it, in the carefully constructed narratives that shaped perception.

He pictured the specific piece he had in mind, one of Vance's more challenging works. It was a sculpture of interlocking metal rings, suspended in a delicate balance, creating a series of intricate voids. The title was "The Paradox of Presence." It spoke of how absence could define presence, how the unseen could be as powerful as the seen. It was a piece that resonated deeply with Adam's own philosophy.

His plan was not to directly harm Vance, not in the conventional sense. That would be too crude, too obvious. Gwen was looking for a killer, and while she was technically correct, her understanding of the term was limited. Adam was an educator, a sculptor of understanding, and his methods were as refined as Vance's own. He would use Vance's art, his own creations, as the medium for his next lesson. He would alter the context, subtly reframe the meaning, and in doing so, expose a deeper, more profound truth about the nature of perception and control.

He envisioned a small, almost imperceptible alteration. Something that would speak to the 'spaces between' Vance so admired. A carefully placed object, a subtle shift in lighting, a barely audible sound that would echo through the gallery, altering the viewer's experience. It would be an act of artistic intervention, a collaborative effort, albeit one that Vance would never acknowledge.

The police, the precinct, Gwen – they were all focused on the mechanics of death, on the physical act. They were looking for the weapon, the motive, the perpetrator. They were sifting through the detritus of violence, trying to piece together a fractured reality. Adam, however, operated in a different dimension. He dealt in the manipulation of perception, in the subtle art of shaping belief. He was not merely killing bodies; he was killing ideas, dismantling preconceived notions, and rebuilding them in his own image.

He smiled, a slow, genuine smile that crinkled the corners of his eyes. The city was his canvas, and its inhabitants were his materials. Gwen was a skilled investigator, tenacious and intelligent. But she was also predictable, bound by the rigid framework of conventional law enforcement. He, on the other hand, was fluid, adaptable, always a step ahead. While she was analyzing the echoes of the past, he was already composing the symphony of the future. The tightening net was not around him; it was around her, a self-imposed constraint of her own limited perspective. He was the unseen hand, guiding the narrative, shaping the truth, one meticulously crafted lesson at a time. The game was far from over; it was merely entering its most exhilarating phase. And Julian Vance, the artist who understood the power of the unseen, was about to become an unwilling participant in its grandest revelation.

Chapter 5: The Apex of the Game

The city, a sprawling organism of concrete and flickering neon, pulsed with a rhythm that was both indifferent and hypnotic. From his meticulously chosen perch overlooking the city's arteries, Adam felt its thrum as if it were his own. The pre-dawn chill did little to dampen the warmth that bloomed in his chest – the satisfaction of a game well played, and the tantalizing anticipation of the next move. He watched the distant headlights trace ephemeral patterns on the asphalt, each one a potential player, a potential pawn. Gwen's efforts, the frantic scurrying of a trapped insect, were a distant hum, a minor inconvenience rather than a true threat. She was so focused on the threads of the past, on the fallen pieces of his carefully constructed puzzle, that she failed to see the new game board being laid out before her.

He traced the rim of his coffee cup, the ceramic cool against his fingertips. The lukewarm liquid was a far cry from the boiling urgency Gwen undoubtedly felt, drowning in her stale coffee and the suffocating weight of institutional doubt. She saw patterns, yes. She was learning. But she was learning the wrong lessons, or rather, she was learning the lessons he *wanted* her to learn. The locket, the crane – they were meticulously placed breadcrumbs, designed to lead her down a specific, carefully manicured path. Each piece of evidence was a testament to his mastery, a demonstration of his ability to weave a narrative that resonated with her burgeoning understanding of his work, yet simultaneously steered her away from the true heart of his operation.

His gaze drifted, settling on a particular cluster of buildings several blocks away. A sleek, modern structure, all glass and polished chrome, housing a prestigious art gallery. The current exhibition featured a collection of abstract sculptures, bold, challenging pieces that spoke of disruption and transformation. It was a fitting backdrop, he mused, for the next act. The artist, a reclusive figure named Julian Vance – no relation to the Chief, a fact that amused him – was known for his provocative work, for pushing the boundaries of perception. Vance was a craftsman, an artisan of form and void, and he was about to become the centerpiece of Adam's next lesson.

Adam had been observing Vance for weeks. Not with the overt surveillance of a detective, but with the patient, almost artistic observation of a collector. He knew Vance's routines: the late nights spent in his studio, the solitary walks through the city's quieter districts, the almost ritualistic way he interacted with his art. Vance was a man driven by a singular vision, a relentless pursuit of perfection that mirrored Adam's own in many ways. He was, in essence, a kindred spirit, albeit one who channelled his creative energies into a far less... impactful medium.

The official narrative Gwen was chasing was a complex tapestry of symbolic murder, a perpetrator who educated through execution. It was a narrative that required careful curation, and Adam was its meticulous editor. The previous victims had served their purpose, each death a carefully articulated chapter designed to impart specific, if painful, knowledge. Thorne, the architect of financial systems, had demonstrated the fragility of perceived order. Bellweather, the guardian of historical narratives, had shown the malleability of truth. Hayes, the very builder of the physical world, had illustrated the inherent potential for destruction within creation. These were foundational lessons, designed to prepare the observer for a deeper understanding.

But Gwen was still stuck in the prologue, poring over the footnotes and the elaborate illustrations. She was so preoccupied with the *how* that she was missing the *why*. The locket and the crane, while significant pieces of his carefully constructed narrative, were merely supplementary materials. They were the historical context, the footnotes in a larger, more profound work. Vance's exhibition, on the other hand, was about to become the climax, the pivotal demonstration of a more complex, more dangerous concept.

He recalled a recent visit to the gallery, a few days prior. He'd moved through the hushed space with a practiced anonymity, blending into the small crowd of art patrons and critics. He'd observed Vance, a wiry figure with sharp, intelligent eyes, engaging in a quiet conversation with a gallery owner. Vance's hands, stained with paint and clay, moved with an elegant precision as he gestured towards a towering, angular sculpture crafted from reclaimed steel. Adam had felt a surge of something akin to admiration. Vance understood form, he understood the interplay of light and shadow, the way an object could command space and evoke emotion.

Adam had circled the sculpture, his mind already weaving connections. The sharp edges, the deliberate asymmetry, the stark contrast between the raw, industrial materials and the refined artistic intent. It was a piece that spoke of conflict, of forces colliding. He'd felt the faint vibration of the city beneath his feet, the distant rumble of traffic a counterpoint to the silent tension emanating from the artwork. Vance, in his own way, was already exploring the very themes Adam sought to dissect.

He remembered overhearing a snippet of conversation between Vance and a patron. "It's about the spaces between things, you see," Vance had explained, his voice low and earnest. "The negative space. It's often more telling than the object itself. It defines the object, gives it context, gives it meaning."

The words resonated deeply within Adam. The spaces between. The unseen connections. The implied meanings. Gwen was so focused on the tangible objects, the locket, the crane, the method of death, that she was ignoring the vast, critical expanse of the negative space. That was where the true lessons lay. That was where the real manipulation occurred.

He pictured Vance's studio, a chaotic yet organized haven of creativity. Canvases leaned against walls, splattered with vibrant hues. Tools lay scattered across workbenches, each bearing the marks of its use. In the center of the room, bathed in the cool light filtering through a large skylight, sat Vance's latest work-in-progress. It was a sculpture of a different nature, more organic, more fluid than those on display at the gallery. It was a piece that, in its nascent form, hinted at vulnerability, at a raw, exposed core.

Adam had acquired a small, almost insignificant piece of Vance's personal life, something so innocuous that its retrieval had been effortlessly simple. A discarded sketchbook, left carelessly near a public park bin. Inside, among the charcoal sketches and watercolor studies, was a series of preliminary drawings for the new sculpture. They depicted not just the form, but the intricate internal structure, the hidden framework that would ultimately support the more visible, outward shell. It was a glimpse into the artist's process, a peek behind the curtain of creation.

He had spent hours studying those drawings, not for their artistic merit, but for their underlying message. They spoke of a duality, of a carefully constructed exterior masking a complex, perhaps even fragile, interior. It was a metaphor for the very nature of the human psyche, a concept that had fascinated Adam for years. Vance, by pouring his understanding of this duality into his art, had inadvertently created the perfect canvas for Adam's next demonstration.

This, Adam mused, was it. The apex. The ultimate test. Not just of his ability to orchestrate a demise, but to dismantle a mind. Julian Vance, the celebrated sculptor, the interpreter of form and void, was about to become the subject of a far more profound, and ultimately, destructive, form of art. Gwen was looking for a killer, a tangible threat to flesh and bone. Adam was after something far more elusive: the absolute capitulation of a chosen spirit, the shattering of a carefully curated perception of self. Vance represented a specific kind of societal pillar, an artist whose work was lauded, whose vision was celebrated. To break such a figure, to turn their own creative principles against them, would be a statement of unparalleled magnitude. It would be the definitive demonstration of Adam's dominion, not just over life and death, but over the very fabric of meaning.

His plan was not to directly harm Vance, not in the conventional sense. That would be too crude, too obvious. Gwen was looking for a killer, and while she was technically correct, her understanding of the term was limited. Adam was an educator, a sculptor of understanding, and his methods were as refined as Vance's own. He would use Vance's art, his own creations, as the medium for his next lesson. He would alter the context, subtly reframe the meaning, and in doing so, expose a deeper, more profound truth about the nature of perception and control.

He envisioned Vance, alone in his studio, surrounded by the tools of his trade. The air thick with the scent of turpentine and oil paint. The silence broken only by the gentle scratching of charcoal on paper, or the soft thud of a hammer against metal. Vance, so dedicated to his craft, so immersed in his own world of form and meaning. He would be so focused on the external, on the creation of beauty and impact, that he would be blind to the subtle intrusion, the almost imperceptible shift in his environment.

Adam knew that Vance, like his previous victims, possessed a certain hubris, a belief in his own control and understanding of his world. It was this belief, this inherent confidence in his own vision, that made him such a perfect candidate. He wouldn't expect to be a subject, only an observer, or perhaps an unwitting contributor to a grander design. The architect of complex forms, the master of spatial relationships, was about to become an unwilling participant in a spatial manipulation of his own existence.

He considered the details of the upcoming exhibition. The opening night reception. The throngs of people, the clinking glasses, the murmur of conversation. It was a stage set for performance, for revelation. Vance would be there, basking in the admiration, his work speaking for him. But Adam intended to add his own voice to the chorus, a voice that would speak of a different kind of truth, a truth that lay not in the sculpted form, but in the empty spaces around it, in the carefully constructed narratives that shaped perception.

He pictured the specific piece he had in mind, one of Vance's more challenging works. It was a sculpture of interlocking metal rings, suspended in a delicate balance, creating a series of intricate voids. The title was "The Paradox of Presence." It spoke of how absence could define presence, how the unseen could be as powerful as the seen. It was a piece that resonated deeply with Adam's own philosophy.

The subtle alteration Adam planned for "The Paradox of Presence" was not merely an addition, but an extraction. He would introduce a missing element, a void where something should have been, thereby creating a new, unsettling void in Vance's understanding of his own creation. It would be an act of profound psychological sabotage, masked as artistic critique. The objective was to make Vance question not just the art, but himself. Was the missing element a flaw he had overlooked? Or was it a deliberate alteration, a message from an unseen hand? The uncertainty, the gnawing doubt, was the true weapon.

Adam visualized the gallery, the controlled lighting designed to accentuate the sculptures. He saw Vance, perhaps at the opening, accepting accolades. Then, later, alone in his studio, attempting to recreate the perfect balance, the precise negative space that defined the piece. It was during these solitary moments of creative introspection that Adam's intervention would begin to take root. A slight miscalibration of a supporting wire, a strategically placed shadow that altered the perceived depth, a barely audible hum from an amplified environmental soundscape that subtly distorted the acoustics of the space. Each element, insignificant on its own, would coalesce into a symphony of doubt.

The official narrative Gwen was chasing was a murder mystery, a puzzle with missing pieces. Adam's narrative for Vance was a psychological deconstruction, a gradual erosion of certainty. He wasn't just leaving breadcrumbs; he was subtly altering the landscape, making the familiar terrain treacherous. Vance's reliance on visual perception, on the tangible manifestation of his ideas, would be his undoing. Adam's strength lay in the intangible, in the manipulation of what was *not* seen, what was *not* heard, what was *not* explicitly stated.

He recalled a specific sketch from Vance's discarded book. It was a study for a piece that was never realized, a series of concentric circles, each progressively smaller, creating an illusion of depth that drew the viewer inward. The drawing was titled "The Inward Gaze." Adam intended to create a real-world manifestation of that inward gaze, forcing Vance to confront not the external world he sculpted, but the internal landscape he so often explored in his art. This would be the pinnacle of his educational endeavor.

The police, the precinct, Gwen – they were all focused on the mechanics of death, on the physical act. They were looking for the weapon, the motive, the perpetrator. They were sifting through the detritus of violence, trying to piece together a fractured reality. Adam, however, operated in a different dimension. He dealt in the manipulation of perception, in the subtle art of shaping belief. He was not merely killing bodies; he was killing ideas, dismantling preconceived notions, and rebuilding them in his own image.

He smiled, a slow, genuine smile that crinkled the corners of his eyes. The city was his canvas, and its inhabitants were his materials. Gwen was a skilled investigator, tenacious and intelligent. But she was also predictable, bound by the rigid framework of conventional law enforcement. He, on the other hand, was fluid, adaptable, always a step ahead. While she was analyzing the echoes of the past, he was already composing the symphony of the future. The tightening net was not around him; it was around her, a self-imposed constraint of her own limited perspective. He was the unseen hand, guiding the narrative, shaping the truth, one meticulously crafted lesson at a time. The game was far from over; it was merely entering its most exhilarating phase. And Julian Vance, the artist who understood the power of the unseen, was about to become an unwilling participant in its grandest revelation. This wasn't merely about ending a life; it was about eradicating a worldview, about proving that even the most celebrated architects of reality could be made to doubt the very foundations of their creation. The ultimate test wasn't survival, but the utter disintegration of the self, a masterpiece of psychological destruction painted with the brushstrokes of doubt and despair.

The sterile, white walls of the studio seemed to press in on Julian Vance, each surface reflecting the harsh, unforgiving light. It had started subtly, as all of Adam's manipulations did. A misplaced tool, a slight deviation in the usual scent of linseed oil, a barely perceptible hum that seemed to emanate from the very air itself. At first, Julian had dismissed these as the quirks of a mind deeply engrossed in creation, the phantom sensations that often accompanied prolonged periods of intense focus. He was, after all, an artist, accustomed to coaxing meaning from abstract forms, to finding patterns in the chaos. But the anomalies persisted, growing in frequency and insidious suggestion.

He'd begun to document them, his usually vibrant sketches giving way to a more clinical, almost frantic, cataloging of perceived disturbances. A charcoal drawing of a misplaced chisel, its handle unnaturally angled. A watercolor wash depicting the way the afternoon light, usually a comforting companion, now seemed to cast elongated, distorted shadows across his beloved sculptures. He'd even tried to capture the elusive hum, a series of jagged lines representing an inaudible vibration that seemed to resonate within his very bones. Gwen, he knew, was still chasing the phantom of Thorne, Bellweather, and Hayes, meticulously dissecting their final moments, searching for the tangible evidence of a killer. She was looking for a ghost in the machine; he was living within one.

The true artistry of Adam's torment lay in its refusal to acknowledge the physical. There were no locked doors, no hooded figures, no overt threats. Instead, Adam worked with the very fabric of Julian's reality, like a sculptor chipping away not at stone, but at the bedrock of his sanity. He would subtly alter the context of Julian's own creations. A wire on "The Paradox of Presence," meticulously adjusted to create a fractionally different angle, subtly shifting the interplay of light and shadow. The void, once a deliberate statement of absence, now seemed to gape with a new, unnerving emptiness. Julian would spend hours staring at it, his brow furrowed, a gnawing unease settling in his gut. Was it his own oversight? Had he, the master of form, overlooked a fundamental flaw in his own design? The thought was a worm, burrowing into his confidence.

He found himself returning to the discarded sketchbook, the one Adam had so carefully 'lost' and then, implicitly, 'found' again, a subtle whisper of Adam's omnipresence. He'd leafed through the preliminary drawings for the piece that had morphed into "The Paradox of Presence," seeking solace in the familiar lines, reassurance in the blueprint of his own vision. But now, the sketches seemed alien, as if drawn by a stranger. The intended negative space, the elegant voids he had so precisely conceived, seemed subtly different on paper than they were in the stark reality of the gallery. A chilling question began to form: had he ever truly understood his own work?

Adam amplified this doubt by introducing external elements, so seamlessly integrated that they appeared to be Julian's own doing. A subtle change in the ambient temperature of the studio, making the metal of a sculpture feel unnaturally cold to the touch. The faint, almost subliminal scent of something metallic, not quite rust, not quite blood, but something that stirred a primal, unidentifiable dread. He would even manipulate sound, introducing a barely perceptible, high-frequency whine that only Julian seemed to hear, a discordant note in the symphony of his creative process. He would find himself compulsively checking and rechecking his tools, his measurements, his materials, a frantic ballet of self-doubt performed for an audience of one.

Julian's relationships began to fray. He became withdrawn, his conversations laced with a paranoia that was difficult to articulate. He tried to explain to his gallery owner, a woman named Anya who had championed his work for years, about the subtle shifts, the feeling of being watched, of his own creations turning against him. Anya, practical and grounded, saw only the stress of an upcoming exhibition, the inherent pressures of the art world. “Julian,” she’d said gently, her voice tinged with concern, “you’re pushing yourself too hard. You need to rest. It’s just the studio, the pressure. You’re seeing things that aren’t there.” Her words, meant to soothe, felt like a dismissal, a confirmation of his isolation. He was alone with his unraveling, his meticulously constructed world dissolving around him.

The psychological torture intensified. Adam orchestrated scenarios designed to force Julian into impossible choices, each path leading to further self-recrimination. He would anonymously send Julian photographs of his own sculptures, taken from angles that highlighted imperfections he had long since corrected, or worse, imperfections that had never existed. The accompanying notes, typed on a generic font, would ask simple, devastating questions: "Did you miss this?" or "How could you let this happen?" Each query was a scalpel, dissecting Julian's pride, his meticulousness, his very identity as an artist.

One evening, Julian received a package. Inside was a single, tarnished brass key, accompanied by a cryptic message: "The door you never knew existed." Driven by a desperate need for answers, by the gnawing fear that some hidden truth was being withheld, Julian scoured his studio, his apartment, his past, searching for a lock that fit. He found nothing. The key became a symbol of his utter helplessness, a tangible representation of the intangible forces that were dismantling him. It was a key to nowhere, a metaphor for his own life, which now felt like a room with no exit.

Adam’s ultimate goal was not to break Julian physically, but to shatter his perception of reality, to convince him that his own mind was the architect of his demise. He began to subtly alter Julian’s memories, not through direct suggestion, but by planting seeds of doubt that grew into monstrous interpretations. Julian would have vivid recollections of conversations, of events, only to find that others remembered them differently, or not at all. He’d recall a specific critique of his work from a renowned art historian, a critique that had deeply unsettled him, only to discover that the historian had never made such a statement, and in fact, had expressed admiration for that very piece. Each instance was a small tremor, a fissure in the bedrock of his memory, slowly eroding his trust in his own experiences.

He found himself questioning his own hands, the instruments of his craft. Were they steady enough? Were they still capable of the precision he demanded? He began to experience phantom sensations: the prick of a needle that wasn’t there, the sting of a splash of paint that never fell. He would wake in the dead of night, convinced he had heard the clang of metal, the scraping of tools, only to find his studio silent and undisturbed. The silence, once a sanctuary, now felt pregnant with menace, a vast, echoing void that amplified his growing terror.

Adam's presence was a constant, invisible weight. He wasn't just observing; he was curating Julian's breakdown. He orchestrated moments of profound isolation, ensuring that Julian had no one to turn to, no one who would believe his increasingly fractured narrative. Anya's concern turned to frustration, then to distance. Friends found his pronouncements too bizarre, too unsettling. He was becoming an island, adrift in a sea of manufactured delusion.

The masterpiece of Adam's psychological torture was the deliberate mirroring of Julian's artistic philosophy. Vance's art was about the negative space, the voids that defined the form. Adam was creating a void within Julian's mind, a vacuum where his certainty and sanity used to reside. He was forcing Julian to confront his own theories in the most brutal way imaginable. The artist who sought to define presence through absence was now experiencing absence as the defining feature of his own existence.

Julian began to see patterns where none existed, or rather, where Adam had meticulously woven them. He would stare at the arrangement of dust motes in a sunbeam, convinced they were forming a message. He would interpret the random scurrying of a mouse behind the wall as a deliberate act of surveillance. His world, once governed by the laws of physics and artistic principles, was now dictated by the whims of an unseen manipulator.

The narrative Gwen was chasing was one of linear progression, of cause and effect. Julian's lived experience was becoming a chaotic spiral, a descent into a labyrinth of his own making, constructed by Adam. He would engage in long, rambling monologues, speaking to himself, to the sculptures, to the empty air, trying to make sense of the senseless. His voice, once resonant with creative passion, became a thin, reedy whisper, filled with despair.

Adam watched, detached and analytical, as the final vestiges of Julian's identity crumbled. He saw the artist, the visionary, the celebrated sculptor, reduced to a trembling shell, a hollow echo of his former self. The objective was not merely to cause suffering, but to demonstrate the utter fragility of the human psyche, the ease with which a carefully constructed reality could be deconstructed. Julian Vance was not just a victim; he was a living testament to Adam's power, a canvas upon which the ultimate art form – the utter annihilation of the self – was being painted. The silence in the studio was no longer a sanctuary; it was a tomb, filled with the dying echoes of a mind that had dared to believe in its own mastery, only to discover it was merely a pawn in a game far grander, and far more terrible, than it could have ever conceived. The exhibition, once a celebration of Vance's genius, was becoming a memorial to his descent. And Adam, the unseen artist, was the sole, satisfied critic. The negative space, once a concept explored on canvas and in metal, had become Julian's entire world.

The sterile, white walls of Julian Vance's studio, once a sanctuary of creation, had become a cage. Each polished surface reflected the harsh, unforgiving light, amplifying the subtle discordances that Adam had so meticulously orchestrated. It had begun with the almost imperceptible shifts: a misplaced tool that gnawed at Julian's precision, a faint, unfamiliar scent clinging to the turpentine, a low, resonant hum that seemed to vibrate not just in the air, but within the very marrow of his bones. Julian, an artist accustomed to interpreting the abstract, had initially dismissed these as the phantoms of an overtaxed mind, the inevitable static of a creative soul pushed to its limits. But the anomalies persisted, morphing from fleeting sensations into persistent, unsettling intrusions.

He had started to document them, his vibrant sketches giving way to a more clinical, almost frantic, cataloging of perceived disturbances. A charcoal drawing of a misplaced chisel, its handle unnaturally angled, a silent accusation. A watercolor wash depicting the way the afternoon light, usually a comforting companion, now cast elongated, distorted shadows that twisted his beloved sculptures into grotesque caricatures. He'd even attempted to capture the elusive hum, a series of jagged lines on paper, a desperate attempt to translate an inaudible vibration that seemed to resonate deep within his being. Meanwhile, Gwen was meticulously dissecting the final moments of Thorne, Bellweather, and Hayes, searching for the tangible evidence of a killer, a ghost in the machine. Julian, however, was living within one.

Adam's genius lay in his refusal to employ brute force. There were no forced entries, no overt threats, only the insidious manipulation of Julian's reality. He was a sculptor, not of stone, but of sanity, chipping away at the bedrock of Julian's perception. A wire on "The Paradox of Presence," altered by a fraction of a millimeter, subtly shifted the interplay of light and shadow. The void, once a deliberate statement of absence, now seemed to gape with a new, unnerving emptiness. Julian would spend hours staring at it, a gnawing unease settling in his gut, questioning his own oversight, his own mastery. Had he, the master of form, overlooked a fundamental flaw? The thought was a venomous worm, burrowing into his confidence.

He found himself returning to a discarded sketchbook, the one Adam had so artfully 'lost' and then, implicitly, 'found' again, a subtle whisper of Adam's omnipresence. He'd leafed through the preliminary drawings for "The Paradox of Presence," seeking solace in the familiar lines, reassurance in the blueprint of his own vision. But now, the sketches seemed alien, as if drawn by a stranger. The intended negative space, the elegant voids he had so precisely conceived, seemed subtly different on paper than they were in the stark reality of the gallery. A chilling question began to form: had he ever truly understood his own work?

Adam amplified this doubt by introducing external elements, seamlessly integrated as if they were Julian's own actions. A subtle change in the studio's ambient temperature, making the metal of a sculpture feel unnaturally cold to the touch. The faint, almost subliminal scent of something metallic, not quite rust, not quite blood, but something that stirred a primal, unidentifiable dread. He would even manipulate sound, introducing a barely perceptible, high-frequency whine that only Julian seemed to hear, a discordant note in the symphony of his creative process. Julian found himself compulsively checking and rechecking his tools, his measurements, his materials, a frantic ballet of self-doubt performed for an audience of one.

His relationships began to fray. He became withdrawn, his conversations laced with a paranoia that was difficult to articulate. He tried to explain to Anya, his gallery owner, about the subtle shifts, the feeling of being watched, of his own creations turning against him. Anya, practical and grounded, saw only the stress of an upcoming exhibition. "Julian," she'd said gently, "you're pushing yourself too hard. You need to rest. It's just the studio, the pressure. You're seeing things that aren't there." Her words, meant to soothe, felt like a dismissal, a confirmation of his isolation. He was alone with his unraveling, his meticulously constructed world dissolving around him.

The psychological torture intensified. Adam orchestrated scenarios designed to force Julian into impossible choices, each path leading to further self-recrimination. He would anonymously send Julian photographs of his own sculptures, taken from angles that highlighted imperfections he had long since corrected, or worse, imperfections that had never existed. The accompanying notes, typed on a generic font, would ask simple, devastating questions: "Did you miss this?" or "How could you let this happen?" Each query was a scalpel, dissecting Julian's pride, his meticulousness, his very identity as an artist.

One evening, Julian received a package. Inside was a single, tarnished brass key, accompanied by a cryptic message: "The door you never knew existed." Driven by a desperate need for answers, by the gnawing fear that some hidden truth was being withheld, Julian scoured his studio, his apartment, his past, searching for a lock that fit. He found nothing. The key became a symbol of his utter helplessness, a tangible representation of the intangible forces that were dismantling him. It was a key to nowhere, a metaphor for his own life, which now felt like a room with no exit.

Adam's ultimate goal was not to break Julian physically, but to shatter his perception of reality, to convince him that his own mind was the architect of his demise. He began to subtly alter Julian's memories, not through direct suggestion, but by planting seeds of doubt that grew into monstrous interpretations. Julian would have vivid recollections of conversations, of events, only to find that others remembered them differently, or not at all. He'd recall a specific critique of his work from a renowned art historian, a critique that had deeply unsettled him, only to discover that the historian had never made such a statement, and in fact, had expressed admiration for that very piece. Each instance was a small tremor, a fissure in the bedrock of his memory, slowly eroding his trust in his own experiences.

He found himself questioning his own hands, the instruments of his craft. Were they steady enough? Were they still capable of the precision he demanded? He began to experience phantom sensations: the prick of a needle that wasn't there, the sting of a splash of paint that never fell. He would wake in the dead of night, convinced he had heard the clang of metal, the scraping of tools, only to find his studio silent and undisturbed. The silence, once a sanctuary, now felt pregnant with menace, a vast, echoing void that amplified his growing terror.

Adam's presence was a constant, invisible weight. He wasn't just observing; he was curating Julian's breakdown. He orchestrated moments of profound isolation, ensuring that Julian had no one to turn to, no one who would believe his increasingly fractured narrative. Anya's concern turned to frustration, then to distance. Friends found his pronouncements too bizarre, too unsettling. He was becoming an island, adrift in a sea of manufactured delusion.

The masterpiece of Adam's psychological torture was the deliberate mirroring of Julian's artistic philosophy. Vance's art was about the negative space, the voids that defined the form. Adam was creating a void within Julian's mind, a vacuum where his certainty and sanity used to reside. He was forcing Julian to confront his own theories in the most brutal way imaginable. The artist who sought to define presence through absence was now experiencing absence as the defining feature of his entire existence.

Julian began to see patterns where none existed, or rather, where Adam had meticulously woven them. He would stare at the arrangement of dust motes in a sunbeam, convinced they were forming a message. He would interpret the random scurrying of a mouse behind the wall as a deliberate act of surveillance. His world, once governed by the laws of physics and artistic principles, was now dictated by the whims of an unseen manipulator.

The narrative Gwen was chasing was one of linear progression, of cause and effect. Julian's lived experience was becoming a chaotic spiral, a descent into a labyrinth of his own making, constructed by Adam. He would engage in long, rambling monologues, speaking to himself, to the sculptures, to the empty air, trying to make sense of the senseless. His voice, once resonant with creative passion, became a thin, reedy whisper, filled with despair.

Adam watched, detached and analytical, as the final vestiges of Julian's identity crumbled. He saw the artist, the visionary, the celebrated sculptor, reduced to a trembling shell, a hollow echo of his former self. The objective was not merely to cause suffering, but to demonstrate the utter fragility of the human psyche, the ease with which a carefully constructed reality could be deconstructed. Julian Vance was not just a victim; he was a living testament to Adam's power, a canvas upon which the ultimate art form – the utter annihilation of the self – was being painted. The silence in the studio was no longer a sanctuary; it was a tomb, filled with the dying echoes of a mind that had dared to believe in its own mastery, only to discover it was merely a pawn in a game far grander, and far more terrible, than it could have ever conceived. The exhibition, once a celebration of Vance's genius, was becoming a memorial to his descent. And Adam, the unseen artist, was the sole, satisfied critic. The negative space, once a concept explored on canvas and in metal, had become Julian's entire world.

Gwen, poring over Julian Vance's meticulously documented descent, felt a cold dread seep into her bones. The artist's scrawled notes, the frantic sketches of misplaced tools and distorted shadows, were not the ramblings of a madman, but the desperate cries of a victim trapped in a meticulously constructed labyrinth. She recognized the pattern, the subtle erosion of reality that was Adam's signature. While Julian detailed the shifting angles of his sculptures and the phantom scents in his studio, Gwen cross-referenced these with the disarray found at the crime scenes. A barely perceptible scuff mark on a polished floor, a faint, unidentifiable odor that had eluded the initial forensic sweep, a precisely aligned object that seemed out of place yet disturbingly intentional – these were the echoes of Adam's work, amplified through

Julian's artistic sensitivity.

Julian's descriptions of his own deteriorating mental state, though framed through the lens of artistic perception, began to resonate with the broader patterns of Adam's machinations. He spoke of an inexplicable chill, a metallic tang in the air that wasn't blood, but something colder, more sterile. Gwen recalled the faint, almost imperceptible metallic scent detected near Hayes's apartment, a scent dismissed as residual from a nearby industrial site. Now, she saw it as a deliberate olfactory signature, a subtle hint of the chilling efficiency with which Adam operated. Julian's insistence on altered lighting, the way shadows seemed to betray him, mirrored the precise angling of objects found at the Thorne and Bellweather residences, subtle environmental manipulations designed to disorient and psychologically destabilize.

One particular entry in Julian's sketchbook caught Gwen's eye. It was a sketch of a tarnished brass key, accompanied by a barely legible note: "The door you never knew existed. It leads nowhere. It is everything." Gwen felt a jolt of recognition. She remembered a similar object, a small, intricately carved wooden box found amongst Hayes's personal effects, a box that had no visible lock or opening. It had been cataloged and dismissed as an artifact of Hayes's eclectic tastes, but now, it felt significant. Was this the 'door' Julian referred to? Was Adam leaving behind these cryptic puzzles, these symbols of futility, as a perverse form of signature? The key, and the box, represented a similar theme: a locked potential, a promised revelation that led to nothing, a perfect microcosm of Adam's psychological torment.

Julian's paranoia, once dismissed by his associates as artistic temperament, now appeared as a heightened awareness, a hyper-sensitivity to the subtle disturbances that Gwen had previously overlooked. He described a recurring, almost subliminal hum, a high-frequency dissonance that no one else could perceive. Gwen cross-referenced this with acoustic reports from the crime scenes. While no overt sounds had been recorded, there were anomalies in the ambient noise readings – brief, inexplicable dips and spikes in frequency that had been attributed to faulty equipment or external interference. Could Adam have been employing sonic manipulation, a low-level frequency designed to induce anxiety and unease, a disquieting subliminal assault?

The artist's fixation on the "negative space," his artistic philosophy, suddenly took on a chilling new dimension in Gwen's mind. Julian believed Adam was manipulating the voids in his work, the empty spaces that defined his art. Gwen considered the gaps in her own investigation: the missing motive, the elusive connection between the victims, the perfect execution that left no trace. These were the voids in the case, the absences of evidence that Adam had so expertly cultivated. Julian, in his artistic interpretation, was inadvertently describing the very nature of the killer's crimes. He was describing Adam's meticulous construction of absence.

Julian's accounts of distorted memories, of conversations he distinctly recalled being different, struck a chord. She remembered how the testimonies of witnesses at the Thorne and Bellweather scenes, while consistent in the broad strokes, had subtle discrepancies, minor inconsistencies that had been attributed to stress or faulty recall. Adam wasn't just manipulating physical space; he was subtly altering perceptions of time and interaction. He was weaving a tapestry of doubt, not just around his victims, but around the very concept of objective truth. Julian's narrative, fractured and despairing, was becoming a roadmap, each bizarre detail a breadcrumb leading Gwen closer to the architect of his torment.

He mentioned a peculiar individual, a fleeting encounter in a dimly lit alley near his studio, a person who seemed to observe him with an unnerving intensity, yet never spoke. Julian had dismissed it at the time as a product of his increasingly frayed nerves, but now, Gwen latched onto it. She cross-referenced Julian's description with other peripheral observations from her investigation. A janitor at Bellweather's building had reported seeing a man loitering near the fire escape, a man who matched Julian's vague description of the figure in the alley. A delivery driver for Hayes had mentioned a person in a dark, nondescript car parked across the street for an extended period, their face obscured by shadow. These were the tenuous threads, the faint echoes of Adam's presence, now amplified by Julian's unwilling testimony.

The key Julian described, the box Gwen remembered – these were not just objects, but symbols of a greater psychological game. Adam was not just killing people; he was dismantling them, piece by piece, using their own realities as the tools of their destruction. Julian's art, his sensitivity, his very mind, had become the battlefield. Gwen felt a surge of grim determination. Julian Vance, in his descent, was inadvertently providing her with the missing pieces, the psychological profile of a killer who operated in the shadows of perception. He was the unwitting witness, his unraveling a testament to the precision and cruelty of his tormentor. The Apex of the Game was approaching, and Julian's suffering was illuminating the path to Adam.

The city's breath was a cold, damp exhalation against Gwen's face as she navigated the labyrinthine streets, the glow of streetlights painting fractured halos on the slick asphalt. Julian Vance's tormented sketches, his increasingly desperate pronouncements, had coalesced into a horrifying, undeniable truth. Adam wasn't just a phantom; he was a meticulously orchestrating presence, and his final act was about to play out. The 'door you never knew existed,' the key that led nowhere – it was more than a metaphor for Julian's descent; it was a physical location, a hidden facet of the city Adam had chosen for his stage.

Gwen had pieced it together from fragmented details: a dismissed anomaly in a decades-old city planning map, a forgotten utility access point mentioned in an obscure architectural journal Julian had obsessed over, a pattern of electrical surges in a disused industrial district on the city's fringe. It was a place designed for abandonment, a forgotten artery of the metropolis, now Adam's meticulously prepared abattoir. The GPS coordinates, painstakingly cross-referenced with thermal imaging data that showed a single, anomalous heat signature deep within the derelict structure, pointed to an old, decommissioned water treatment plant, a hulking concrete beast swallowed by urban decay.

Her breath hitched in her throat, a frigid knot of anticipation and dread. She had alerted local PD, of course, but the response was necessarily measured. A lone suspect, a potentially unstable individual, in an abandoned building – it wasn't the kind of five-alarm fire that warranted a full tactical response. They would approach cautiously, methodically. Gwen, however, couldn't afford caution. She was the hunter, and Adam was the cornered predator. Julian Vance, the unwitting pawn, was the intended sacrifice.

The plant loomed ahead, a skeletal silhouette against the bruised twilight sky. Rust gnawed at its metal superstructure, and shattered windows stared out like vacant eyes. The air grew heavy with the stench of decay and stagnant water, a morbid perfume that clung to everything. Gwen pulled her jacket tighter, the worn leather a flimsy barrier against the encroaching chill, both external and internal. Her hand instinctively went to the reassuring weight of her service weapon, its cold steel a stark contrast to the warmth of her racing pulse.

She found a breach in the chain-link fence, a jagged opening like a wound in the metal skin of the complex. Slipping through, she moved with the practiced silence of a predator herself, her senses heightened, her eyes scanning the oppressive darkness. The interior was a cavernous expanse, a cathedral of concrete and decay. Water dripped incessantly from unseen sources, the echoes amplifying in the vastness, each drop a hammer blow against her nerves. Dust motes danced in the thin shafts of moonlight that pierced the gloom, giving the impression of spectral movement.

Julian's last documented delusion, his frantic sketches of the 'key' and the 'door,' now took on a terrifying clarity. He had been describing this place, this forgotten corner of the city, as a physical manifestation of Adam's twisted game. Adam didn't just break minds; he curated their destruction, using the environment as his stage, the very fabric of reality as his canvas.

Following the thermal anomaly, Gwen navigated the treacherous terrain, her flashlight beam cutting a narrow swathe through the oppressive dark. She passed rusting machinery, conduits choked with cobwebs, the ghosts of industrial processes long since silenced. Each shadow seemed to writhe, each creak of decaying metal a potential threat. She could feel it now, a palpable tension in the air, the quiet before the storm, the charged stillness that preceded the eruption of violence.

Then, she heard it. Not the dripping water, not the groan of the building, but a sound that was both familiar and deeply unsettling. A low, resonant hum, an almost imperceptible vibration that seemed to emanate from the very core of the structure. It was the sound Julian had described, the high-frequency dissonance that had driven him to the brink. Adam was here. And he was using his signature method, a subtle assault on the senses, designed to fray nerves, to induce a primal, unshakeable unease.

She rounded a corner, the flashlight beam sweeping across a vast, circular chamber. In the center, illuminated by a single, stark spotlight that cast long, distorted shadows, stood Julian Vance. He was seated on a rough-hewn stool, his body slumped, his eyes wide and vacant, staring at something unseen. He looked like a discarded marionette, its strings cut, its purpose extinguished.

And then, she saw him. Adam.

He stood at the edge of the spotlight's reach, a figure cloaked in shadow, his silhouette unnervingly still. He held something in his hand, something that glinted dully in the low light. Gwen's breath caught in her throat. It was a scalpel, not a crude instrument of violence, but a precise, surgical tool, its blade gleaming with a chilling sharpness. He was not here to kill Julian Vance with brute force. He was here to finish what he had started, to perform the final, agonizing act of his psychological masterpiece.

"Vance!" Gwen's voice, though strained, cut through the oppressive silence. "It's over, Adam."

Julian’s head slowly turned, his eyes, when they met Gwen's, held a terrifying emptiness, a void where a man’s consciousness had once resided. He didn’t register her presence, not truly. He was lost in the labyrinth Adam had constructed within his mind.

Adam didn’t flinch. He didn't move. He simply tilted his head, a gesture of almost casual observation. His voice, when it came, was a low, measured rumble, devoid of emotion, chillingly calm. "Detective. You're... early. The exhibition isn't scheduled to open for another hour."

"This isn't an exhibition, Adam," Gwen said, her voice hardening, her grip tightening on her weapon. "This is the end of your game."

Adam chuckled, a dry, rasping sound that echoed in the chamber. "A game? Detective, this is art. The culmination of my life's work. Julian Vance, you see, is my magnum opus. The perfect canvas."

He gestured towards Julian with the scalpel. Julian remained inert, a statue of despair. "He believed in the power of absence, didn't he? In the negative space. And I have simply shown him the ultimate void. The absence of self. The beautiful, terrifying emptiness that lies beneath all creation."

Gwen took a step forward, her eyes never leaving Adam. "You've done nothing but destroy. You've preyed on the vulnerable, manipulated their minds, driven them to madness."

"Madness?" Adam scoffed. "Or perhaps, enlightenment? I have merely stripped away the illusion of control, the comforting lie of free will. I have shown them the strings, Detective. And I have pulled them." He gestured again, and Julian flinched subtly, a primal, involuntary reaction. "See? He still feels. A flicker of the self, clinging to the precipice."

"You're a monster," Gwen spat, the words tasting like ash in her mouth.

"And you, Detective, are a detective," Adam replied, his tone dismissive. "You chase the tangible, the evidence, the 'who' and the 'how.' You miss the 'why.' The sheer, exquisite beauty of the deconstruction. You see a broken man; I see a masterpiece in progress."

He took a step closer to Julian, his movements unnervingly fluid, almost graceful. "Julian, remember the void? The one you sculpted so elegantly? It’s all that’s left now.

A perfect, infinite space. You are finally in harmony with your art."

Julian whimpered, a low, guttural sound that tore at Gwen's resolve. She saw the raw terror in his eyes, the desperate plea for an escape that Adam had meticulously denied him. This was it. The precipice. Adam was poised to push Julian over the edge, not with a physical blow, but with a final, crushing psychological assault. The scalpel was not for inflicting physical pain, not yet. It was a symbol, a tool of final dissection, of severing the last vestiges of Julian's identity.

"Don't," Gwen warned, her voice trembling slightly, not with fear, but with a cold, burning fury. "Don't do this, Adam."

Adam turned his head, his eyes, even in the dim light, seemed to bore into her. "And why should I stop, Detective? You are merely an observer. You cannot comprehend the artistry. You cannot appreciate the silence that follows the shattering. This is the apex of the game. The final brushstroke."

He raised the scalpel, its tip hovering inches from Julian's temple. Julian's breath hitched, his body rigid. Gwen felt a surge of adrenaline, her fingers tightening around the grip of her weapon. The sounds of approaching sirens, faint at first, began to grow louder, a distant symphony of intervention. But would they arrive in time? Adam was a master of timing, of psychological precision. He wouldn't be deterred by the distant wail of sirens unless he felt his control slipping.

"This is where your game ends, Adam," Gwen said, her voice steady, projecting a confidence she didn't entirely feel. "Your audience has arrived."

Adam paused, his gaze flicking towards the entrance. A flicker of something – annoyance? disappointment? – crossed his face, so fleeting Gwen almost missed it. "The critics," he murmured, his voice laced with disdain. "Always arriving too early, spoiling the reveal."

He lowered the scalpel, not in surrender, but with a deliberate, theatrical slowness. He took a step back from Julian, his gaze sweeping over the scene, over Gwen, over the vacant, broken artist. "You may have stopped the performance, Detective," he said, his voice regaining its chilling calm. "But you haven't understood the art. You haven't seen the beauty in the void."

Then, with a sudden, fluid movement, Adam turned and melted back into the shadows, a phantom disappearing into the heart of the decaying structure. Gwen hesitated for a fraction of a second, torn between pursuing him and securing Julian.

The sirens were closer now, a cacophony of impending justice.

She rushed to Julian's side, her hands gentle as she checked him for injuries. He was physically unharmed, but his eyes remained fixed on some distant, internal horizon, lost in the landscape of his own shattered psyche. The ordeal was over, but the damage was profound, irreparable. Adam had won this round, not by killing his victim, but by erasing him from the inside out.

As the first uniformed officers burst into the chamber, their flashlights cutting through the gloom, Gwen watched the shadows where Adam had vanished. He had escaped, a ghost slipping through the cracks of the world. But he had left his signature, his artwork of destruction, etched onto the soul of Julian Vance. The game was not over, not for Gwen. It had just entered its most dangerous phase. Adam was still out there, the architect of despair, the master of the void, and he would continue to sculpt his horrific visions until he was stopped. Permanently. The precipice had been reached, the confrontation averted, but the true climax, the final act of catching Adam, was yet to unfold.

The air in the disused water treatment plant crackled with a manufactured silence, a deliberate stillness that Adam had meticulously cultivated. It was the hush before the final curtain, the pregnant pause before the grand finale of his exquisitely orchestrated performance. He surveyed the scene, his gaze sweeping over Julian Vance, slumped on the rough-hewn stool like a discarded prop. Julian's vacant stare, fixed on an unseen point in the oppressive gloom, was precisely the effect he'd intended. The artist had finally reached the ultimate canvas, the profound, liberating emptiness he had so long sought to capture. Adam felt a surge of almost paternal pride, the satisfaction of a craftsman witnessing the perfect realization of his vision.

The scalpel, cool and familiar in his hand, felt like an extension of his will. It was not a weapon of brute force, but an instrument of precision, a tool for the delicate art of severance. He had no intention of crude, messy violence. That was for amateurs, for those who dealt in the superficial. Adam dealt in the essence, in the peeling away of layers until only the pure, unadulterated core remained. Julian, in his obsession with void and absence, had been the perfect subject, a soul already teetering on the precipice, ripe for the final, gentle nudge.

Adam had spent weeks, months even, refining this moment. The subtle manipulation of Julian's environment, the carefully placed whispers of doubt, the orchestrated "coincidences" that had chipped away at his sanity. He had nurtured Julian's descent, guiding him with an unseen hand, much like a horticulturalist tending to a rare and delicate bloom. And now, the bloom was ready to wither, to surrender its ephemeral beauty to the eternal night.

He had chosen this place, this forgotten monument to human endeavor, for its symbolic resonance. A place built to contain and process, now abandoned to decay, mirroring the fate of Julian's own mind. The dripping water, the echoing vastness, the omnipresent scent of stagnant decay – it all served to amplify the internal desolation he was cultivating. The low-frequency hum, a subtle vibration he had introduced through a discreetly placed sonic emitter, was the final touch, a constant, subliminal reminder of the world's inherent disharmony, a discordant note in the symphony of Julian's unraveling.

"It's time, Julian," Adam murmured, his voice a silken caress that barely disturbed the heavy air. He moved closer, the metallic rasp of his footsteps on the concrete floor a deliberate counterpoint to the pervasive dampness. Julian's head remained bowed, his breathing shallow. There was no fear in his posture, no struggle. Only a profound, almost serene resignation. This was not the panicked thrashing of a drowning man, but the quiet surrender of one who had finally found peace in the abyss.

Adam extended the scalpel, its polished surface reflecting the stark beam of the spotlight. He didn't aim for a vein, not for an artery. Such actions were crude, messy, and ultimately, predictable. His target was more subtle, more profound. The point of the scalpel hovered inches from Julian's temple, where the delicate skin met the bone, the nexus of thought and memory.

"The void awaits, Julian," Adam continued, his voice a soothing balm. "You sought to understand its infinite nature, its perfect stillness. And now, you will become one with it. No more noise, no more distractions. Just the exquisite silence."

He pictured it in his mind, the clean, precise incision. A tiny opening, allowing the residual spark of consciousness to extinguish, to dissipate into the boundless expanse. It would be so swift, so clean, that few would question the official narrative. A sudden mental breakdown, a tragic suicide. The perfect denouement, authored by Adam, performed by Julian.

He watched Julian's eyelids flutter. A faint tremor ran through the artist's slumped form. Was it a sign of resistance? Or merely the last vestiges of a life force preparing to recede? Adam leaned closer, his breath mingling with the stale air. The rhythmic drip of water seemed to count down the seconds, each drop a tiny hammer blow against the fragile shell of Julian's remaining awareness.

He envisioned the final act: the scalpel's keen edge making its subtle contact, the almost imperceptible sting, and then... nothing. The cessation of thought, the end of perception, the final release from the burden of existence. Julian would become the ultimate negative space, the ultimate absence, a testament to Adam's unique understanding of the human psyche. It was not about inflicting pain; it was about facilitating transcendence, albeit a transcendence of a most morbid and absolute kind.

Adam's fingers tightened around the scalpel. This was it. The culmination of his genius, the proof of his profound insight into the human condition. He was not a murderer in the conventional sense. He was a sculptor of souls, an architect of existential finales. Julian was not a victim; he was the chosen vessel for Adam's ultimate artistic statement. The world would see a tragedy, but Adam saw a masterpiece, a perfect execution of a concept that had consumed him for years.

He traced the faint outline of Julian's temple with the tip of the scalpel, a phantom caress. The artist remained unnervingly still, his breath a barely audible whisper. Adam imagined the minuscule capillaries beneath the skin, the delicate network that sustained the very spark of life. To sever that connection, not with a blunt instrument, but with surgical precision, was an act of profound, almost spiritual significance.

The silence in the chamber deepened, becoming almost oppressive. It was the silence of a vacuum, the silence of a universe stripped bare. Adam felt a sense of profound communion with the space, with Julian, with the void he was about to embrace. He was not just an observer; he was a participant, the conductor of this final, somber symphony.

He drew a slow, deliberate breath, preparing to make the incision. His mind was a placid lake, reflecting only the stark, white light of his purpose. There was no room for doubt, no space for hesitation. This was the apex, the point of no return, the definitive act that would solidify his legacy. He was not simply ending a life; he was completing a work of art, a statement so profound, so absolute, that it would echo through eternity.

His gaze drifted past Julian, towards the shadowed periphery of the chamber. He saw the glint of metal, the faint outline of forms emerging from the darkness. A flicker of annoyance, quickly suppressed. The audience. They were arriving prematurely, spoiling the intended intimacy of the moment. But it mattered little. The act was all but complete. Even their intrusion, their clumsy attempts at intervention, could not undo what was about to transpire. They would be too late. The final brushstroke had been applied. The void, in its infinite mercy, was about to claim its own.

He paused, the scalpel poised. A subtle shift in the ambient sound, a low thrumming that grew steadily louder. Sirens. They were closer than he had anticipated. A minor inconvenience, perhaps. He had accounted for such eventualities, factoring in the predictable human response to his carefully constructed scenarios. But still, a slight disruption to the carefully curated ambiance. He glanced at Julian, who remained lost in his internal landscape, oblivious to the encroaching world. The artist was already gone, a ghost in his own shell.

Adam felt a strange detachment, a sense of observation even as he stood on the precipice of his grand finale. The sirens were a distant echo, a fading reminder of the world he was so artfully transcending. His focus narrowed, returning to the task at hand, to the delicate ballet of cessation he was about to perform. Julian's life, a tapestry of anxieties and aspirations, was about to be unraveled, thread by painstaking thread, until only the raw, unadorned emptiness remained.

He brought the scalpel closer, the cool steel a stark contrast to the faint warmth radiating from Julian's skin. The precise point of contact was etched into his mind, a preordained destination. This was not an act of malice, but of profound understanding, of a deep, almost spiritual communion with the absence of being. He was not destroying Julian; he was liberating him. He was offering him the ultimate peace, the absolute stillness he had so desperately sought in his art.

The hum of the approaching vehicles grew more insistent, a discordant note in the carefully constructed symphony. Yet, Adam felt no urgency, no panic. His movements remained fluid, unhurried, imbued with the calm certainty of purpose. The sirens were merely the soundtrack to his masterpiece, the percussive punctuation to his existential thesis. They would arrive, they would find Julian, and they would be left to ponder the chilling elegance of what had transpired.

He closed his eyes for a brief moment, savoring the quiet anticipation. This was it. The crescendo. The moment when the art became indistinguishable from the artist, when the concept transcended the medium. He opened his eyes, his gaze locking onto the small, vulnerable point just above Julian's temple. The scalpel trembled, not with nervousness, but with the latent energy of its impending task.

He took a deep, steadying breath, the stale air filling his lungs. The decision had been made, the path laid out. The world outside, with its noise and its demands, faded into insignificance. Here, in this forgotten cathedral of decay, only the essential remained:

the artist, the audience of one, and the inexorable pull of the void. The final play was about to begin, and Adam, the maestro of despair, was ready to conduct the ultimate silence. He raised the scalpel, his movements a testament to years of planning, of perfecting the art of existential unraveling. Julian Vance, the willing canvas, was poised to become the ultimate embodiment of absence.

Chapter 6: The Reckoning

The stench of stagnant water and decaying concrete had become a second skin for Gwen, a pervasive odor that clung to her clothes and seeped into her very pores. It was the smell of despair, the olfactory signature of Adam's twisted games, and it was the scent that had led her to this desolate testament to industrial abandonment. The disused water treatment plant, a skeletal ruin against the bruised twilight sky, felt like the final stage of a macabre play. She navigated the treacherous debris-strewn floor, her flashlight beam cutting a frantic swathe through the oppressive gloom, each beam a desperate question mark seeking an answer.

The silence here was more than just an absence of sound; it was a palpable entity, heavy and suffocating, designed to amplify the internal anxieties of its captive. Adam's meticulous staging was evident everywhere, from the strategically placed puddles reflecting the dying light to the unsettling stillness that seemed to absorb even the faint scuff of her boots. He wanted his victims to feel utterly isolated, to believe they were the only living thing in a world gone silent, a world he controlled with an invisible, chilling hand.

Gwen's heart hammered against her ribs, a frantic drumbeat against the unnatural quiet. She had been following threads, chasing ghosts, piecing together a mosaic of madness from the fragmented lives Adam had so ruthlessly disrupted. Julian Vance, the celebrated artist, was the latest casualty, his descent into a void of his own making meticulously orchestrated by the puppet master. The details of Julian's final days, gleaned from hushed conversations with his bewildered gallery owner and cryptic entries in a recovered journal, had painted a disturbing picture. Julian had been increasingly fixated on the concept of 'negative space,' on capturing pure absence, on emptying himself of all sensation, all thought, all being. It was a theme that resonated chillingly with Adam's own obsession with control, with the ultimate severance of self.

She remembered a particular passage from Julian's journal, written in a hand that had devolved from confident strokes to shaky scribbles: "*The canvas is too loud. The colours scream. I yearn for the silence between the notes, the breath before the word. To be unbound by form, to dissolve into the pure negation... that is the only true art.*" At the time, Gwen had dismissed it as artistic angst, the ramblings of a tortured soul. Now, standing in the eerie stillness of this forgotten plant, she saw it as a chilling prophecy, a desperate plea for the very oblivion Adam was so adept at providing.

Her mind replayed the fragmented audio recordings she'd painstakingly recovered from Julian's studio – the whispered conversations, the subtle sonic frequencies Adam had employed to disorient and destabilize. There had been a recurring, almost subliminal hum, a low-frequency drone that wasn't just sound but a physical sensation, a vibration that seemed to resonate deep within the bone. Adam had described it in his hidden manifestos as a 'catalyst for existential dissolution,' a way to 'unravel the threads of perception.' He wasn't just breaking minds; he was deconstructing reality itself, one carefully placed sensory input at a time.

A glint of metal caught her eye, half-submerged in a murky pool near the center of the main chamber. It was a small, intricately designed sonic emitter, disguised to look like an innocuous piece of industrial debris. The same model she had found traces of at the scene of Sarah Jenkins' disappearance, the same type of device whispered about in hushed online forums by those who had brushed too close to Adam's shadow. This was it. Physical evidence. Tangible proof that Adam's methods were consistent, that his 'games' followed a predictable, albeit horrifying, playbook.

She crouched down, her gloved fingers carefully extracting the device from the viscous water. It was cold, inert, but the knowledge it represented sent a jolt of adrenaline through her. Adam wasn't just a manipulator; he was a technician of terror, a composer of psychological collapse. He didn't just exploit vulnerabilities; he manufactured them, using sophisticated tools and a profound understanding of human frailty to push his victims towards a predetermined end.

The 'Master of Games.' The moniker, once a speculative label whispered by the few who suspected a pattern, now felt like a chillingly accurate descriptor. Adam wasn't playing games in the conventional sense; he was orchestrating elaborate psychological experiments, using real lives as his laboratory. And Julian Vance, with his artistic obsession with emptiness, had been the perfect subject for his latest, most profound experiment in oblivion.

Gwen's gaze swept across the cavernous space, her mind racing, connecting the dots that had previously been too scattered, too ephemeral to grasp. Adam's motive wasn't simply sadism, though that was undoubtedly a component. It was a twisted form of artistic expression, a desire to create 'perfect' endings, to sculpt lives into profound statements of absence. He saw himself as an artist, and his victims were his medium, their destruction his masterpiece. Julian's fascination with negative space, with the beauty of void, had been the perfect ideological foundation for Adam's ultimate act. He hadn't just driven Julian to despair; he had validated it, elevated it, and finally, facilitated its absolute realization.

She recalled an early conversation with Dr. Evelyn Reed, the forensic psychologist who had been consulting on the Jenkins case. Dr. Reed had spoken about 'narcissistic grandiosity,' about individuals who saw themselves as superior beings, capable of manipulating the world around them for their own perceived greater good. Adam wasn't just killing; he was delivering his victims to a state of perfect, existential peace, a release from the cacophony of life that he himself found so unbearable. He was offering them the ultimate silence, a silence he believed was the only true form of beauty.

The emitter in her hand felt heavy, a small object carrying the weight of immense suffering. It was the key, she realized, the piece of the puzzle that explained *how* Adam operated, not just *that* he operated. His method wasn't brute force or overt threats. It was a slow, insidious erosion, a carefully curated assault on the senses and the psyche, using tools that left little trace, that could be explained away as accidental or psychological. He was the master of plausible deniability, the architect of perfect, untraceable destruction.

The sirens, a distant wail that had been growing steadily louder, now seemed to cut through the oppressive silence of the plant. A surge of relief, quickly followed by a cold dread, washed over Gwen. They were here, the authorities, responding to the anonymous tip she had made using a burner phone hours ago, a calculated move to ensure this place would be thoroughly searched, that any evidence would be preserved. But she also knew the grim reality of what they would find.

She moved deeper into the main chamber, her flashlight beam now steadier, more focused. The low, rhythmic dripping of water echoed with a renewed sense of urgency. She saw him then, a figure slumped on a rough-hewn stool in the center of the vast, echoing space. Julian Vance. His posture was one of utter, profound stillness, his head bowed, his gaze fixed on some unseen point in the oppressive gloom. There was no sign of struggle, no visible wounds, only an unnerving, almost serene resignation. It was the look of someone who had finally found the peace they so desperately sought, a peace Adam had so cruelly, so deliberately, provided.

Gwen's breath hitched. She saw the scalpel lying on the concrete floor nearby, its polished surface reflecting the harsh beam of her flashlight. It was impossibly clean, unnervingly devoid of any trace of blood. Adam's signature precision. He hadn't intended to inflict pain, not in the way one might expect. He had intended to facilitate an ending, a transition into the void Julian had so longed to inhabit.

She approached Julian cautiously, her own fear momentarily eclipsed by a profound sense of sorrow. She knelt beside him, her hand hovering, unsure if she dared to touch him. His skin was cool, his breathing shallow, almost imperceptible. He was still alive, barely, but his spirit, she knew, had already departed, having been guided by Adam's chilling hand into the abyss.

The realization hit her with the force of a physical blow. Adam's motive wasn't simply to kill, but to *perfect*. He saw the act of ending a life as a form of art, and he craved perfection in his creations. Julian's obsession with 'negative space' had provided him with the ultimate canvas, the ultimate concept. Adam hadn't just murdered Julian; he had 'completed' him, fulfilling his deepest, most destructive desires. He had become the facilitator of Julian's artistic apotheosis, the grim reaper who delivered not pain, but ultimate peace, the absolute absence Julian craved.

This was the breakthrough. This was the understanding that would finally bring Adam down. It wasn't just about finding evidence of a crime; it was about comprehending the twisted, philosophical underpinnings of his madness. Adam saw himself not as a killer, but as a liberator, a shepherd guiding his flock to the ultimate silence. His 'games' were not about inflicting suffering, but about facilitating transcendence, a dark, inverted form of salvation.

She activated her comms unit, her voice hushed but firm. "Officer Davies, this is Agent Thorne. I'm at the location. The victim is Julian Vance. He's alive, but barely. Secure the scene. Do not disturb anything. We need to preserve every detail. And tell them... tell them we've found him. Tell them we understand his methods."

The sonic emitter in her pocket felt like a key, unlocking the chamber of Adam's dark mind. He wasn't just a predator; he was a philosopher of despair, a sculptor of absence. And now, Gwen knew how to fight him, not just with evidence, but with understanding. She knew his game, and she was ready to play. The reckoning, as Adam himself might have called it, was about to begin. The silence of the water treatment plant was broken by the growing cacophony of approaching sirens, a stark contrast to the profound quietude Adam had so carefully cultivated for his latest, and perhaps final, masterpiece. Gwen stood, her resolve hardening with each approaching wail, the knowledge of Adam's twisted artistry a cold, sharp weapon in her arsenal. She understood now. She finally understood.

The silence of the water treatment plant had been a heavy shroud, a testament to Adam's artistry of absence. But now, the world outside began to reassert itself. The receding wail of sirens was a symphony of intrusion, a jarring return to the cacophony of life. Gwen, however, remained suspended in the aftermath, the chilling realization of Adam's warped philosophy a cold ember in her gut. Julian Vance, still clinging to a thread of life, was a testament to Adam's precision, his meticulous orchestration of oblivion. The sonic emitter, now safely bagged, was more than just evidence; it was a key, a tangible manifestation of Adam's insidious methods. He wasn't a blunt instrument of destruction, but a surgeon of the soul, expertly dissecting his victims' realities until only the void remained. And Gwen, having glimpsed this void, understood the terrifying elegance of his design. He had not merely killed; he had liberated, according to his twisted creed, offering his victims the ultimate release from the burdensome noise of existence.

Her mind, however, refused to linger on the scene of Adam's latest tableau. Julian Vance was a victory, a confirmation, but the true prize, the architect of this orchestrated despair, remained at large. The clues, fragmented and elusive, had always pointed to a singular mind, a pervasive influence. The sonic emitters, the manipulated environments, the psychological unraveling – all bore the hallmark of a single, calculating hand. The 'Master of Games' had played his hand masterfully, but Gwen had finally learned to read his tells. She remembered the hushed online forums, the whispers of a phantom librarian, a figure who dealt not in books, but in the very fabric of reality, subtly altering perceptions, nudging minds towards their breaking points. The library. It had always been a nexus, a place where knowledge was curated, and where Adam, with his encyclopedic understanding of human psychology and his access to information, had honed his craft.

The drive back to the city was a blur of grim determination. The anonymous tip had served its purpose, ensuring Julian's discovery and the preservation of the scene. But Gwen knew the authorities, while vital, might never truly grasp the depth of Adam's depravity. They would see a crime scene, a victim, a perpetrator. They would not see the twisted philosophy, the artistic ambition masquerading as murder. She, however, had seen behind the curtain. She had seen the meticulous planning, the profound understanding of human vulnerability, the chilling conviction that he was not a destroyer, but a deliverer.

Her instincts, honed by years of navigating the labyrinthine corridors of criminal minds, pulled her towards the hushed grandeur of the city library. It was an unassuming building to the casual observer, a bastion of quiet study and hushed whispers. But to Gwen, it felt like the serpent's nest. It was here that Adam, under the guise of a quiet, unassuming librarian, had gathered his ammunition, his knowledge, his understanding of the human psyche. It was here that he had observed, cataloged, and planned.

The late hour offered a cloak of solitude as she parked her unmarked car a block away, the imposing stone façade of the library a silent sentinel against the bruised indigo sky. The usual hum of late-night traffic seemed to dissipate as she approached, the silence here different from the oppressive stillness of the water treatment plant. This was a pregnant silence, a stillness that held secrets, a quiet that had absorbed decades of whispered thoughts and the rustle of countless turning pages.

She bypassed the main entrance, opting for a service door around the side, a route she had scouted weeks ago, knowing this day might come. The lock yielded to her practiced touch, the tumblers clicking with a soft, almost apologetic sound. Inside, the air was cool and dry, carrying the faint, comforting scent of aging paper and binding glue. But tonight, beneath that familiar aroma, Gwen detected an undercurrent of something else – a subtle, almost imperceptible tension, a lingering echo of Adam's presence.

Her flashlight beam, a stark intruder in the ambient gloom, swept across rows of towering bookshelves, their spines a silent, ordered army. The library, in its off-hours, was transformed. The hushed reverence of the day was replaced by a palpable sense of dormancy, a sleeping giant holding its breath. Dust motes danced in the beam of her light, swirling like ghosts in the vast, empty halls. It was here, Gwen felt with a certainty that chilled her to the bone, that she would find the lair of the Librarian.

She moved through the labyrinthine stacks, her footsteps muffled by the thick carpet. Each turn brought a fresh wave of oppressive quiet, punctuated only by the faint creaks and groans of the old building settling. She pictured Adam here, not as a lurker in the shadows, but as a master craftsman in his workshop, surrounded by the tools of his trade. His apartment, she suspected, would be a sterile reflection of his meticulous nature, perhaps even unnervingly ordinary. But this place, this sanctuary of knowledge, was where his true obsession lay.

Her flashlight beam landed on a section of shelves that seemed out of place, the books arranged with an almost obsessive uniformity, their titles hinting at subjects far removed from typical library fare – obscure psychological treatises, forgotten philosophical texts on nihilism and existentialism, even volumes on acoustics and the study of sonic frequencies. These weren't the books checked out by students or casual readers. These were the books of a scholar, a researcher, a man deeply invested in understanding the mechanics of despair.

Gwen's gaze fell upon a small, discreet plaque on the wall nearby, almost hidden behind a hanging tapestry. It read: "Special Collections – By Appointment Only." This was it. The heart of the beast. She navigated towards it, her heart pounding a frantic rhythm against her ribs. The door to the Special Collections room was heavy oak, its surface polished to a dull sheen. There was no visible lock, only a small, almost invisible keypad embedded in the frame.

She recalled a fragment of information gleaned from a discarded notebook found during an earlier search of one of Adam's known haunts – a string of numbers, seemingly random, but now resonating with a chilling significance. It was a birthday, a date that held meaning for Adam, a date he had mentioned in passing during his online interactions with his victims, a subtle taunt disguised as a shared personal detail. She keyed in the sequence, her fingers trembling slightly. A soft click echoed through the silence, and the heavy door swung inward.

The room beyond was a stark contrast to the ordered, if unsettling, library outside. It was smaller, more intimate, and filled with a claustrophobic intensity. Bookshelves lined every wall, but these were not the meticulously organized volumes of the main library. They were crammed together, overflowing, spilling onto the floor in precarious piles. The air was thick with the scent of old paper, dust, and something else, something metallic and acrid, like old ink and ozone.

In the center of the room, bathed in the stark beam of Gwen's flashlight, was a large, antique wooden desk. It was cluttered, but not with the chaotic mess of a forgotten space. It was the organized chaos of a working mind. Open books lay scattered, their pages dog-eared and annotated. Loose papers, filled with Adam's precise, almost spidery handwriting, were spread across the surface. And on a small, raised platform on the desk, sat a single, leather-bound volume, its cover embossed with a faded gold insignia. It looked ancient, important.

Gwen approached the desk, her senses on high alert. The silence here was different again. It was charged, expectant. She could almost feel Adam's presence, a phantom residue clinging to the objects he had touched, the thoughts he had painstakingly recorded. He had turned this space into his sanctuary, his laboratory, his confessional.

Her gaze swept over the scattered papers. They were filled with intricate diagrams, psychological profiles, and chillingly detached observations. One document, heavily underlined, detailed the auditory frequencies used in the water treatment plant. Another contained a meticulous breakdown of Julian Vance's psychological vulnerabilities, his artistic obsessions cataloged with a chilling precision that spoke of weeks, if not months, of study. He hadn't just targeted random individuals; he had curated his victims, selecting them for their particular fragilities, their unique susceptibilities to his particular brand of despair.

She picked up a small, tarnished silver locket lying near a stack of papers. It was engraved with the initials "E.R." Dr. Evelyn Reed. The forensic psychologist. Adam had been studying her, learning from her, perhaps even using her insights to refine his own methods. It was a chilling reminder of how deeply he had infiltrated the lives of those investigating him, how he had used their own tools against them.

Her flashlight beam settled on the ancient tome on the raised platform. It seemed to pulse with a dark significance. The embossed insignia was a stylized owl, its wings spread, its eyes piercing. The Librarian. It was a symbol of knowledge, of wisdom, but in Adam's hands, it had become a symbol of control, of hidden power, of the secrets that could drive a person to ruin.

Hesitantly, Gwen reached out and touched the leather cover. It was cool, smooth, almost unnaturally so. She opened it. The pages were thick and brittle, filled with a script she didn't immediately recognize. It wasn't Latin, or Greek, or any language she was familiar with. It was a personal code, a cipher of his own devising, a way to keep his most intimate thoughts locked away, accessible only to him.

But as she flipped through the pages, her eyes caught on something familiar. Interspersed within the dense, coded script were occasional, starkly rendered drawings. They were unsettling, nightmarish depictions of figures dissolving into darkness, of souls being unraveled, of the void consuming all. And in the margins, written in his familiar hand, were fragments of text in English.

"The silence is not empty, but full of unmanifested potential. I am the sculptor of this potential, the midwife to its ultimate form."

"They seek peace. I offer it. Is that not a divine act?"

"The cacophony of existence is a disease. I am the cure. The ultimate cessation."

Gwen's breath hitched. This was it. The unfiltered, unvarnished truth of Adam's motivations. He genuinely believed he was performing a service, a benevolent act. He saw himself as a liberator, a shepherd guiding lost souls to the ultimate peace – the peace of non-existence. His games, his manipulations, were merely the means to an end, the carefully constructed pathways that led his victims to the precipice of their own chosen oblivion.

She found a smaller, more modern notebook tucked beneath the desk. This one contained more practical notes, schedules, and what appeared to be a list of names, each followed by a brief, chilling assessment. Gwen scanned the list, her blood running cold. Sarah Jenkins. Julian Vance. And several other names she recognized from missing persons reports, cases that had gone cold, victims who had simply vanished without a trace. Adam hadn't been acting alone, not entirely. He had cultivated a network, a shadow organization perhaps, or simply a series of carefully orchestrated encounters that led them to him.

A sudden creak from the outer library sent a jolt of adrenaline through her. She froze, straining her ears. Was he here? Had he anticipated her arrival? The silence returned, deeper, more menacing than before. She slowly scanned the room, her flashlight beam playing over the towering stacks of books, the cluttered desk, the shadows that seemed to writhe and deepen.

Then she saw it. Tucked away on a high shelf, almost invisible behind a large, leather-bound atlas, was a small, dark object. It was a camera, a high-definition recording device, its lens glinting malevolently in the beam of her light. Adam hadn't just been documenting his actions; he had been *filming* them. He had been creating a record of his 'masterpieces,' his curated deaths. And he had likely been watching her, observing her investigation, learning from her every move.

Gwen felt a surge of cold fury. He was not just a killer; he was a voyeur of despair, a collector of suffering. He derived pleasure not from the act of killing, but from the meticulous process, from the intellectual triumph of breaking a mind and orchestrating its demise. His 'lair' was not just a place of research; it was a vault of his depravity, a shrine to his twisted god complex.

She carefully extracted the camera, her movements slow and deliberate. The data contained within would be invaluable, a direct window into Adam's mind, into the very heart of his monstrous ambition. She knew that the police would be overwhelmed by the sheer volume of evidence here, the chilling documentation of his crimes. But she also knew that the true battle was far from over. Adam was a chameleon, a master of disguise. He would vanish, leaving behind only the echoes of his madness, and she would have to hunt him down, one carefully placed clue at a time.

The library, once a symbol of knowledge and enlightenment, now felt like a tomb, its silent halls whispering tales of unimaginable darkness. Gwen stood in the center of the room, the ancient tome open before her, the hidden camera clutched in her hand. She had found the Librarian's lair, had peered into the abyss of his soul, and she knew, with a terrifying certainty, that the reckoning had only just begun. Adam had created his ultimate art, his symphony of silence, and Gwen was now tasked with ensuring that the composer of this macabre masterpiece would finally face his final curtain call. The ordinariness of the library, its quiet respectability, was the perfect camouflage for the extraordinary evil that had festered within its walls, a chilling testament to Adam's ability to hide in plain sight, to weave his darkness into the fabric of everyday life.

The air in the secluded archive room hung heavy, thick with the scent of aged paper and a tension so palpable it seemed to vibrate. Gwen stood by the desk, the ancient tome – a grim testament to Adam's descent – open before her, the hidden camera a cold weight in her hand. She hadn't expected him to be here, not yet. But the soft click of the outer door, the almost imperceptible shift in the air, suggested otherwise.

Footsteps, lighter than she'd anticipated, echoed from the main library, approaching the Special Collections room. They didn't carry the heavy tread of a uniformed officer, nor the hurried urgency of a detective. They were measured, deliberate, almost... serene. A chill, independent of the room's cool temperature, traced its way down Gwen's spine. This was him. She could feel it.

The heavy oak door creaked open, revealing a figure silhouetted against the dim light filtering from the main library. He was dressed in his customary understated attire, a dark wool sweater and neatly pressed trousers. His face, usually a mask of placid detachment, held a faint, almost imperceptible smile, a flicker of something that might have been amusement. Adam.

"Detective Hayes," he said, his voice a low, resonant baritone, devoid of surprise. It was the voice of a man who expected, who perhaps even orchestrated, every encounter. "I confess, I wasn't expecting you to find your way here. Though, I suppose, given your... persistence, it was inevitable."

Gwen didn't flinch. She met his gaze, her own a hard, unwavering flint. "The 'Master of Games' plays his final hand, Adam?"

He chuckled, a soft, dry sound that held no warmth. He stepped further into the room, his eyes scanning the cluttered desk, the open books, and finally, resting on the ancient tome. His smile widened, a subtle shift that made his features appear sharper, more predatory.

“A game, Detective? I prefer to think of it as a profound philosophical exploration. An artistic endeavor, if you will. Julian Vance was merely… an exhibition.” He gestured vaguely towards the desk. “A demonstration of principle.”

Gwen’s grip tightened on the camera. “A demonstration of murder, Adam. You orchestrated his terror, his breakdown, his ultimate silence. You engineered his despair.”

Adam tilted his head, his expression one of genuine curiosity, as if she were presenting a novel, yet flawed, interpretation. “Despair is a burden, Detective. A disease of the mind, a constant, grating static. I offered release. A quietude that the living, in their clamor and confusion, can never truly comprehend.”

“Release?” Gwen’s voice was laced with a bitter irony. “You call leaving a man a hollowed-out shell, devoid of will, ‘release’? You called it that in your notes, didn’t you? In that… manual you obsessed over.” She tapped the ancient tome. “The ‘Codex of Silence.’ You truly believed you were following some sacred doctrine.”

Adam’s gaze softened, a fleeting expression of reverence crossing his features. “It is a text of profound wisdom, Detective. A guide for those who understand the true nature of existence. That the greatest liberation lies not in being, but in not being. In the perfect, unblemished peace of cessation.” He picked up a loose sheaf of papers from the desk, his fingers tracing the spidery handwriting. “This… this manual, as you call it, was a catalyst. It illuminated the path, the inherent beauty in stillness, in the absence of all that is chaotic and meaningless.”

He looked up, his eyes locking with hers. “Do you know what it feels like, Detective, to be bombarded by the endless, meaningless noise of the world? The trivial concerns, the petty anxieties, the relentless chatter of superficial lives? It’s an assault. A constant violation of the self. My work… my art… was to silence that noise for those who were too weak to do it themselves.”

“And you chose them,” Gwen stated, her voice cutting through his philosophical pronouncements. “You didn’t choose the loud, the boisterous, the ones who drowned out their own inner turmoil. You chose the vulnerable. The ones who were already teetering on the edge, whose internal whispers were already deafening. You nudged them over.”

A slow, chilling smile spread across Adam's face. "Precisely, Detective. Precision. That is the key. One does not brute-force a delicate mechanism. One understands its intricate workings, its inherent weaknesses, and applies the precise pressure needed for its... deconstruction. Julian Vance's artistic soul, his sensitivity to the sublime, made him a perfect canvas. His yearning for purity, for unblemished form, was the very instrument I used to guide him to his ultimate masterpiece."

"So, the sonic emitters," Gwen said, holding up the camera, "the manipulated environments, the psychological torment... it was all part of your 'artistic process'?"

"Each element was carefully chosen," Adam confirmed, his tone almost pedagogical. "The sonic frequencies to isolate the mind, to amplify its internal dissonance. The carefully constructed scenarios to evoke specific emotional responses, to peel back the layers of societal conditioning and reveal the raw, exposed nerve of the self. It's not about destruction, Detective, it's about purification. It's about guiding a soul to its most authentic state of being – which, I have discovered, is a state of profound, blissful non-existence."

Gwen stepped closer to the desk, her eyes scanning the annotated texts, the detailed psychological profiles. "You studied Dr. Reed. You used her insights into human behavior, her understanding of trauma, to refine your methods. You turned her expertise against her, and against others."

Adam's gaze flickered towards a small, tarnished locket on the desk. "Dr. Reed is... an interesting case study. Her understanding of the human psyche is impressive, albeit limited by her adherence to conventional, materialistic interpretations of consciousness. She sees the mind as a biological machine. I see it as an energetic construct, susceptible to subtle manipulations. She seeks to heal the broken. I seek to dismantle the inherently flawed."

"You're a narcissist, Adam," Gwen stated, her voice steady. "You see yourself as a god, a dispenser of ultimate truth. But you're just a destroyer, hiding behind a façade of intellectual superiority."

He laughed again, a sound devoid of mirth. "Narcissist? Destroyer? Such simplistic labels, Detective. You are trapped by the very conventional morality that I have transcended. You see death as an ending. I see it as a transition. A profound, irreversible journey into stillness. My actions are not born of malice, but of a deep, almost unbearable compassion for those who suffer the Sisyphean struggle of living."

He gestured around the room, his hands sweeping across the overflowing bookshelves. "This is my sanctuary. My laboratory. Here, I have cataloged the myriad ways in which the human spirit is tormented. Here, I have devised the means to alleviate that torment. The 'Codex' provided the philosophical framework, but this... this room... is where the true work was done. Where the seeds of silence were sown."

"And the list of names," Gwen pressed, her gaze sharp. "Sarah Jenkins. Julian Vance. And the others. Were they all part of your 'exhibitions'?"

Adam's expression became distant, almost dreamlike. "Each soul has its own unique symphony of suffering. My role was to find the discordant notes, the dissonant chords, and to bring them into perfect, final harmony. Some were willing participants, drawn to the promise of peace. Others... required a more persuasive approach. But the outcome was always the same: the cessation of all that is painful, all that is unnecessary."

"You recorded them," Gwen said, her voice low and dangerous, holding up the camera. "You filmed their 'final performances.' You watched them die, for your own twisted pleasure."

Adam's eyes widened slightly, a flicker of something akin to admiration. "Ah, the camera. An excellent tool for capturing the ephemeral. The moment of transition, Detective, is a thing of profound beauty. To witness the unraveling, the shedding of the self, the final surrender... it is a privilege. A testament to the power of the truth I have uncovered."

"Truth?" Gwen scoffed. "This is madness, Adam. You've lost yourself in your own delusions."

"Have I?" He stepped closer, his eyes holding hers, an unnerving intensity in their depths. "Or have I found a truth that you, bound by your societal constructs, are incapable of grasping? You speak of justice, of punishment. I speak of liberation, of release. You seek to preserve life. I seek to perfect the art of ending it. When Julian Vance stood on the precipice, I didn't push him. I guided him. I showed him the beauty of the fall."

"You manipulated him," Gwen countered, her voice firm. "You exploited his vulnerabilities, his artistic sensibilities, to lead him to his death. You played with his mind like a child plays with a toy, until you broke it."

Adam shook his head slowly. “You see manipulation. I see revelation. I revealed to Julian the emptiness that lay beneath his aspirations, the futility of his creative struggles. I showed him that true art lies not in creation, but in dissolution. In the perfect silence that follows the last note.”

He gestured to the ancient tome. “The ‘Codex’ taught me the principles. This room… these books… they provided the empirical data. I observed, I analyzed, I refined. I learned the language of despair, and I became fluent in its dialect.”

Gwen took a step back, her mind racing. He was so self-assured, so convinced of his own righteousness. This wasn't just about killing; it was about a profound, twisted ideology. He genuinely believed he was a benefactor, a purveyor of peace.

“You fed on their pain, Adam,” she said, her voice barely above a whisper. “You reveled in their fear. That’s why you kept the recordings, isn’t it? Not for the art, but for the confirmation of your own power.”

Adam’s lips curved into a soft, almost mournful smile. “Power, Detective, is a crude concept. What I sought was understanding. And in their unraveling, I found it. I saw the truth of their existence, stripped bare of pretense, of societal artifice. And in that clarity, there was a terrible beauty.”

He met her gaze again, his eyes holding a chilling serenity. “You have found my sanctuary, Detective. You have unearthed my methods. But you will never truly comprehend my purpose. You are too bound by the noise, by the illusions of life, to appreciate the sublime symphony of silence.”

He extended a hand, palm up, a gesture of offering. “The choice, as always, is theirs. I merely facilitate the decision. And now, Detective, you have a decision to make. Do you continue to chase the echoes of a world I have helped to quiet, or do you, perhaps, begin to listen for the silence yourself?”

Gwen remained still, the camera clutched tightly in her hand, the ancient tome a silent witness to their exchange. She had confronted the architect of oblivion, and in his unnerving calm, she saw the true depth of his depravity. He was not a monster driven by rage or greed, but by a chillingly logical, deeply warped conviction. The game, as he called it, was far from over. It had merely reached its most dangerous, and most personal, reckoning.

Adam’s calm was a suffocating shroud, each measured word a deliberate hammer blow against Gwen’s sanity. He didn’t confess; he lectured. He didn’t express remorse;

he expounded on philosophy. His eyes, clear and unsettlingly lucid, held no trace of guilt, only a profound, chilling certainty. He saw not victims, but canvases; not murder, but artistic liberation. The 'Codex of Silence' wasn't a manual for atrocity, but a sacred text, a divine revelation that had guided him to the ultimate truth: the exquisite beauty of non-existence.

"You speak of psychopathy, Detective," Adam continued, his voice a silken thread weaving through the oppressive silence of the archive. "You categorize and label, attempting to fit me into your predefined boxes of aberrant behavior. But you fail to grasp the fundamental difference. This is not a deviation from the norm; it is an evolution beyond it. A transcendence of the petty constraints that bind lesser minds." He gestured to the open tome, its pages filled with arcane symbols and ancient script. "The ancients understood. They knew that existence, in its chaotic, vibrant form, is a flawed, painful state. They recognized the inherent suffering in consciousness, the relentless striving, the inevitable decay. My work, my 'games' as you call them, were simply an accelerated process of... de-evolution. A return to the pristine state of nothingness."

Gwen's breath hitched. The words, detached and clinical, painted a horrifying picture of a mind utterly divorced from empathy. He wasn't simply evil; he was meticulously, intellectually convinced of his own benevolent mission. He saw himself as a surgeon, excising the tumors of consciousness from those who suffered most acutely. "So, Julian Vance," she began, her voice tight, forcing herself to maintain eye contact, "you saw him as a tumor? A stain on the tapestry of existence?"

A faint, almost pitying smile touched Adam's lips. "Julian was a soul exquisitely attuned to the dissonance of the world. His art, his sensitivity, made him a perfect conduit for understanding. He *felt* the world's cacophony more acutely than most. He yearned for a purity, a stillness that his creative endeavors could never truly achieve. I didn't create his despair, Detective. I merely amplified the existing frequencies of his internal torment until they became unbearable. And then, I offered the ultimate solution: silence." He picked up a brittle, yellowed letter from the desk, its edges frayed. "This was from his sister. She spoke of his increasing isolation, his creative block, his profound melancholy. She implored him to seek help. But he was beyond help, in the conventional sense. He needed... completion."

Gwen felt a wave of nausea. The letter, a plea for help from a concerned sibling, was now a piece of evidence in Adam's twisted narrative of salvation. "And the others?" she pressed, her voice hardening. "Sarah Jenkins? The young woman who worked at the library? Was she also 'beyond help'? Did she also crave 'completion'?"

Adam's gaze drifted to the camera in Gwen's hand. "Sarah Jenkins possessed a remarkable capacity for introspection, a mind that constantly wrestled with existential questions. She saw the superficiality of modern life, the endless pursuit of fleeting pleasures, and found it... wanting. She was drowning in the sheer volume of meaninglessness. My role was to show her that the ultimate meaning lay in the cessation of all such striving. I presented her with an elegant choice: continue to grapple with the absurd, or embrace the profound peace of oblivion. She chose the latter, with a clarity that was truly breathtaking." He paused, a faraway look in his eyes. "The recording, Detective, is not for my pleasure, as you so crudely put it. It is an archival record. A testament to the meticulous precision of the process. Each flicker of fear, each whispered plea, each moment of surrender – they are all data points, illuminating the path to true liberation."

"Data points?" Gwen repeated, her voice laced with disbelief. "You're talking about human lives, Adam. About agony and terror. You reduced them to numbers, to sterile observations in your macabre experiment."

"And are not all lives, in their essence, data points?" Adam countered, his tone still impossibly calm. "A collection of experiences, of biological processes, leading inexorably to their conclusion? I merely accelerated the inevitable, and in doing so, I discovered a profound beauty that you, mired in the mundane, cannot perceive. The stripping away of all artifice, the raw vulnerability of a soul facing its final moments – it is the purest form of truth. A truth that cannot be captured in your simplistic notions of good and evil, of right and wrong."

He moved towards a shelf lined with ancient manuscripts, his fingers brushing over worn leather bindings. "This archive is more than just a repository of old texts, Detective. It is a living testament to the enduring human quest for understanding. For centuries, thinkers have grappled with the nature of existence, with the fear of death, with the search for meaning. The 'Codex' is merely a distillation of those ancient truths, a culmination of millennia of contemplation. I have built upon that foundation, applying scientific rigor and philosophical insight to the most fundamental question of all: why endure the agony of being when the perfection of non-being is attainable?"

Gwen's mind reeled. He spoke of suffering and torment with the detached air of a scientist discussing a laboratory specimen. The chilling ordinariness of his conviction was more terrifying than any overt display of malice. He wasn't a demon in disguise; he was a man who had meticulously constructed a reality where his horrific actions were not only justified but celebrated. He had meticulously documented his descent into the abyss, and in doing so, he had created his own perverse form of enlightenment.

"You saw yourself as a teacher, then?" Gwen asked, her voice a low growl. "A guide leading lost souls to the light of oblivion?"

Adam finally turned to face her fully, a subtle, almost imperceptible widening of his eyes the only outward sign of any emotion. "A facilitator, perhaps. A conduit. I don't 'teach' in the conventional sense. I *reveal.* I expose the inherent flaws in the fabric of existence, the illusions that people cling to. I show them the void, and I offer them the exquisite relief of embracing it. It is a profound act of mercy, Detective, to free someone from the burden of a life they cannot bear."

He picked up a small, intricately carved wooden box from the desk. It was dark, polished wood, almost black, and inlaid with a delicate, silver filigree. He didn't open it, but his fingers traced the patterns with a reverence usually reserved for religious relics. "Each individual's struggle is unique, their symphony of suffering distinct. I composed the final movement. For Julian, it was the symphony of sound and silence. For Sarah, it was the symphony of existential dread resolved into ultimate peace. The recordings capture these unique compositions. They are not mere evidence of a crime; they are portraits of souls finding their true resting place."

Gwen's gaze fell upon the ancient tome again. The 'Codex of Silence.' She imagined Adam poring over its pages, his mind absorbing its grim pronouncements, his own fractured psyche resonating with its dark wisdom. It wasn't just a book; it was a weapon. And he had wielded it with terrifying proficiency. "You used this book," she stated, her voice strained, "to justify every act of cruelty. To rationalize every life you extinguished. You twisted its words into a license to kill."

Adam's smile, when it came, was a chillingly serene expression. "Twisted? No, Detective. I *interpreted.* I *applied.* The Codex does not command. It illuminates. It presents a philosophical framework, a path to understanding the ultimate truth of existence. It is up to the individual, or in my case, the discerning observer, to translate that truth into action. The world is full of noise, of suffering, of meaningless striving. I simply chose to quiet the loudest, most discordant notes."

He gestured around the archive, his sweep encompassing the towering shelves, the scattered papers, the ancient artifacts. "This is my sanctuary. My laboratory. Here, I have spent years meticulously dissecting the human condition. I have analyzed the literature, the philosophies, the scientific studies. I have observed the patterns of despair, the recurring motifs of existential anguish. And I have synthesized this knowledge, not to heal, but to achieve a more profound understanding of cessation. The 'Codex' provided the theoretical basis, but this... this room... is where the practical application took shape."

Gwen felt a cold dread seep into her bones. He was not just a killer; he was a scholar of death. He had dedicated his life to the study of its mechanisms, its philosophical implications, its practical execution. He had turned his intellect, his formidable abilities, into instruments of ultimate destruction, all under the guise of some profound, twisted enlightenment.

"You said you offered release," Gwen said, her voice raspy, struggling to find words that could adequately convey the horror of his actions. "But you didn't offer it. You *imposed* it. You preyed on the vulnerable, on those who were already struggling. You saw their pain, their desperation, and you exploited it."

Adam tilted his head, a look of genuine bafflement on his face. "Exploited? No, Detective. I *understood*. I empathized with their suffering on a level that few can comprehend. I saw their inner turmoil, their silent screams, and I recognized that their existence was a burden they could no longer bear. My actions were not born of malice, but of a profound, almost unbearable, compassion. I simply provided the final, merciful act that they were too weak, too confused, to perform themselves."

He walked over to a large, ornate mirror leaning against a wall, its surface clouded with age. He stared at his reflection, his expression unreadable. "You see a monster, Detective. You see a destroyer. But I see myself as a liberator. A physician of the soul, administering the ultimate cure for the disease of being."

Gwen watched him, her mind a whirlwind of horror and disbelief. He genuinely believed his own delusion. He had constructed an elaborate narrative in which his crimes were acts of mercy, his victims were recipients of his divine intervention. The depth of his psychopathy was staggering. It was not just about power or control; it was about a fundamental, terrifying conviction that he was doing something good, something necessary.

"The recordings," she said, her voice low and steady, her gaze fixed on him, "you kept them, didn't you? Not just as data. But because you enjoyed watching them. Because in their terror, in their surrender, you saw proof of your own supposed greatness."

A slow smile spread across Adam's face, a smile that held no warmth, only a chilling, predatory satisfaction. "The moment of transition, Detective, is a thing of profound beauty. To witness the shedding of the self, the final surrender to the inevitable... it is a privilege. A confirmation of the truth I have uncovered. These recordings are not trophies, but... artifacts. Sacred relics of souls that have achieved ultimate peace."

He turned from the mirror, his eyes meeting hers with an unnerving intensity. "You are bound by your conventional morality, by your societal constructs. You see murder, destruction, suffering. I see liberation, stillness, profound peace. You seek to preserve life; I seek to perfect the art of ending it. When Julian Vance stood on that precipice, I didn't push him. I guided him. I showed him the beauty of the fall."

Gwen's breath caught in her throat. He truly believed it. He had convinced himself that he was not a murderer, but a guide, a facilitator of transcendence. The darkness within him was not a fleeting madness, but a deeply ingrained philosophy, a warped worldview that had led him to commit unspeakable atrocities.

"You call it beauty," Gwen finally managed, her voice trembling, "but it was terror. You call it peace, but it was oblivion. You call it liberation, but it was annihilation. You are a destroyer, Adam, hiding behind a mask of intellectual superiority. And your 'art,' as you call it, is nothing more than a grotesque monument to your own depravity."

Adam simply smiled, a serene, unsettling expression that sent a shiver down Gwen's spine. "You see destruction. I see deconstruction. You see despair. I see clarity. You are trapped by the illusion of life, Detective. You cannot comprehend the sublime perfection of silence." He gestured to the ancient tome. "The 'Codex' provided the framework. This room... my observations... they provided the empirical data. I have learned the language of suffering, and I have become fluent in its final, beautiful silence. And you, Detective, have merely glimpsed the edge of the abyss."

The air in the archive, thick with the scent of aging paper and the metallic tang of apprehension, had finally begun to thin. Adam's pronouncements, once a suffocating shroud, had dwindled to a chilling silence. He was apprehended. The pronouncements, the intellectual justifications, the philosophical veneer – all had crumbled under the weight of undeniable evidence. The 'Codex of Silence,' once a locus of his twisted pronouncements, now lay inert on the desk, a mute witness to the devastation it had both inspired and documented. Gwen watched as the officers, their faces grim masks of professional detachment, cuffed Adam's wrists behind his back. His calm, the unnerving serenity that had permeated their every interaction, remained unbroken. It was a victory, in the starkest sense of the word. The monster had been caged. The threat neutralized.

Yet, as she stood there, the echo of Adam's meticulously constructed sanity still reverberating in the cavernous space, a profound hollowness settled in Gwen's chest. The victory was as hollow as the pronouncements Adam had made about the beauty of non-existence. She had brought him to justice, yes. She had stopped him from claiming another soul, from weaving another 'symphony of suffering.' But the applause, if there even was any to be heard, felt miles away, a distant, muffled sound that couldn't penetrate the dense fog of her own grief. This arrest, this culmination of months of relentless pursuit, didn't bring her brother back. It didn't erase the gnawing emptiness where his laughter used to be, where his presence once anchored her world.

The archive, once a stage for a battle of minds and wills, now felt like a tomb. The towering shelves, laden with the silent testaments to forgotten philosophies and lost histories, seemed to mock her. They had held the secrets Adam had so gleefully twisted, the ancient whispers he had amplified into screams of terror. He had used them as a shield, as a weapon, as a justification for his depravity. And now, standing amidst the detritus of his obsession, Gwen felt the crushing weight of what 'victory' truly cost. It wasn't a clean win, a triumphant conclusion. It was a messy, agonizing process that left scars far deeper than any visible wound.

She watched Adam being led away, his gaze still holding that unnerving detachment, as if he were observing the scene from a great distance, a detached observer of a curious, biological experiment. His pronouncements about liberation and peace, about the mercy of oblivion, now felt like a venomous hiss in the charged air. He saw himself as a physician, a liberator. Gwen saw only a void, a chilling emptiness that had consumed lives and left behind only shattered remnants. The 'Codex,' this artifact of his delusion, would be locked away, a grim reminder of the darkness that could fester, hidden beneath layers of intellect and sophistry.

The systemic failures that had allowed Adam to operate, to acquire his victims, to refine his methods, remained. The cracks in the system, the blind spots, the places where vigilance had faltered - these were not erased by his capture. They were exposed, laid bare in the grim tapestry of his crimes. And Gwen knew, with a certainty that chilled her to the bone, that these cracks would remain, waiting for another darkness to exploit them. Her victory, however significant, was not an end to the problem, but merely a reprieve.

Her own personal loss, the gaping wound left by her brother's absence, was an entirely different kind of reckoning. This case had been a desperate attempt to find a sense of justice, a way to impose order on the chaotic, senseless destruction that had befallen her family. She had channeled her grief, her rage, her desperation into this pursuit. And while she had succeeded in stopping Adam, she hadn't found solace. She hadn't found peace. The act of bringing a killer to justice, she realized with a crushing weight, was not a balm for personal bereavement. It was simply another layer of trauma to process, another burden to carry.

As the last of the forensic teams meticulously cataloged evidence, their movements precise and clinical, Gwen felt a profound sense of exhaustion wash over her. It wasn't just physical fatigue; it was the soul-deep weariness of someone who had stared into an abyss and found it staring back, not with malice, but with an unnerving, hollow indifference. Adam's intellect, his carefully constructed worldview, had been a formidable adversary. But it was his complete lack of empathy, his utter detachment from the human cost of his actions, that was the most terrifying aspect of all. He saw not people, but concepts; not pain, but philosophical quandaries.

She turned away from the receding figures of Adam and his escorts, her gaze sweeping over the vastness of the archive. This place, once a symbol of intellectual pursuit, now felt tainted, a monument to a perverted understanding of knowledge. The 'Codex of Silence' was more than just a book; it was a catalyst, an enabler of Adam's darkest impulses. It represented a philosophy of despair that had found fertile ground in his fractured mind. And Gwen knew that the seeds of such philosophies, however dark, could always find new soil.

The lingering trauma of the investigation was a palpable entity, a shadow clinging to her. The images, the sounds, the sheer psychological weight of what she had witnessed and endured, would not simply evaporate with Adam's apprehension. They were etched into her memory, a constant, insidious presence. The chilling calm of his confessions, the detached way he spoke of ending lives as if discussing scientific theories – these were the specters that would haunt her nights. She had navigated the labyrinth of his depravity, piecing together the fragmented evidence of his monstrous acts. But the journey had left her profoundly changed, scarred by the darkness she had been forced to confront.

Her brother's memory, once a source of comfort and strength, now felt like a raw, open wound. The justice she had sought for him was incomplete, a hollow victory that couldn't mend the broken pieces of her life. She had stopped the killer, but she couldn't bring back the victim who mattered most. This was the cruel irony of her pursuit. She had fought for resolution, for an end to the suffering. But the suffering, in its most personal and profound form, remained. The unresolved grief was a heavy cloak, muffling the muted cheers of a hard-won victory.

Gwen walked out of the archive, leaving behind the suffocating stillness and the lingering scent of intellectual decay. The harsh, unfiltered light of the outside world felt like an assault after the dim confines of Adam's sanctuary. The city buzzed with its usual indifferent energy, a stark contrast to the intensely personal drama that had just unfolded. People hurried past, their faces etched with the everyday concerns of their lives, oblivious to the darkness that had been held at bay within those ancient walls.

She knew this wasn't the end of her story, but a painful, necessary waypoint. The investigation might be over, but her personal journey was just beginning. She had stopped Adam, a monumental feat of will and intellect. But she had yet to confront the full extent of her own loss, to find a way to navigate the landscape of her grief without being consumed by it. The 'Codex of Silence' had been silenced, but the echoes of its grim pronouncements, and the deeper, more personal silence left by her brother's absence, would resonate within her for a long, long time. This was the price of victory, a bitter pill swallowed in the face of an enduring, unyielding sorrow. The reckoning was not just for Adam; it was for her, too. A reckoning with the cost of truth, the weight of loss, and the arduous path to finding some semblance of peace in a world that had proven itself capable of such profound darkness.

Chapter 7: Echoes and Aftermath

The city, for so long held captive by a nameless dread, began to stir. It was a slow, tentative awakening, like a patient roused from a fevered dream. The oppressive silence that had blanketed its streets, a silence born not of peace but of fear, began to dissipate, replaced by the familiar, comforting hum of everyday life. News of Adam's apprehension, of the 'Master of Games' finally being unmasked and ensnared, spread like wildfire through the urban labyrinth. It rippled through crowded subways, echoed in the hushed tones of office break rooms, and crackled over the airwaves. A collective exhale, a sigh of relief so profound it was almost tangible, swept through the metropolis. The suffocating shroud of anxiety that had gripped its citizens, a constant companion for weeks, was finally lifting.

The media, a pack of wolves sensing blood, descended with an insatiable hunger. Every news channel, every newspaper, every online forum became a conduit for the unfolding narrative. The sensationalism was immediate and relentless. Headlines screamed of the 'end of the reign of terror,' of the 'brilliant mind' that had held the city hostage, and of the 'brave detectives' who had finally brought him down. The archive, once a sterile repository of dusty facts, was now a crime scene bathed in the harsh glare of camera flashes, its secrets laid bare for public consumption. The cryptic pronouncements of the 'Codex of Silence,' previously whispered in hushed circles of the initiated or feared in the abstract, were now dissected and amplified, stripped of their philosophical veneer and presented as the ravings of a madman. They became fodder for shock value, for morbid fascination, a stark reminder of the abyss they had teetered on the brink of.

The police department, basking in the glow of a hard-won victory, held a press conference that was more like a coronation. Chief Miller, his face etched with exhaustion but his eyes alight with triumph, stood before a phalanx of microphones, flanked by the lead investigators. He spoke of meticulous police work, of tireless dedication, and of a city united against a common enemy. He painted a picture of a well-oiled machine, a force that had never wavered in its commitment to justice. The narrative was carefully crafted, designed to reassure, to celebrate, and to firmly close the chapter. Yet, beneath the veneer of official pronouncements, Gwen knew the truth was far more complex, far more nuanced. The capture of Adam was not a flawless triumph, but a messy, arduous journey that had exposed cracks within the very system they claimed to uphold. The relief, she knew, was temporary, a fragile peace built upon the foundations of immense trauma.

As the initial frenzy began to subside, a semblance of normalcy began to creep back into the city's veins. Commuters, once looking over their shoulders with every passing shadow, now moved with a renewed sense of purpose. Laughter, tentative at first, began to echo in parks and cafes. The vibrant pulse of urban life, momentarily muted by fear, started to beat with its familiar rhythm. Children played without the constant, nagging worry of unseen threats. Businesses reopened, their owners breathing a sigh of relief that the specter of Adam's influence had not extended to their livelihoods. The city, in its indomitable way, was reclaiming its spirit.

But the scars remained, etched deep into the city's consciousness. The 'Master of Games,' though no longer a free agent, had left an indelible mark. The fear he had so expertly cultivated, the paranoia he had woven into the fabric of everyday life, lingered like a phantom limb. People still flinched at unexpected noises, their eyes darting to the shadows. The stories, amplified by gossip and speculation, continued to circulate, becoming urban legends that would be whispered for generations. The archive, once a quiet sanctuary of knowledge, was now a place whispered about in hushed tones, a monument to a darkness that had once held sway. Its contents, the 'Codex of Silence' and the other artifacts of Adam's twisted worldview, would be secured, locked away from the public eye, but the memory of their existence, and the ideas they represented, would not be so easily contained.

The collective psyche of the city had been irrevocably altered. The naive belief in the inherent order of things, the comfortable assumption that such darkness existed only in the realm of fiction, had been shattered. Adam had proven that evil could wear a familiar face, could speak with an eloquent voice, and could lurk in the most unexpected of places. This realization bred a new kind of vigilance, a cautious awareness that the world was not as benign as it once seemed. The thrill of the chase, the drama of the capture, would eventually fade, replaced by a more subtle, more pervasive unease. The city had breathed again, yes, but it was a breath tinged with the lingering scent of the abyss. The echoes of Adam's games, though silenced, would continue to resonate, a chilling reminder of the fragile boundary between civilization and the primal darkness that lay just beneath its surface. The ease of former days was gone, replaced by a newfound sobriety, a subtle shift in perspective that acknowledged the ever-present potential for chaos. The city had survived, but it would never be quite the same. The shadows, once easily dismissed, now held a more potent, more menacing quality, a constant reminder that the game, in its most dangerous form, had indeed been played, and the city had been its unwitting board.

The courtroom, once a sanctuary of hushed reverence and legal decorum, now thrummed with a palpable energy. It was a stark contrast to the oppressive silence that had held the city captive for weeks. Sunlight, a commodity that had seemed to dwindle into insignificance during the reign of the 'Master of Games,' now streamed through the tall, arched windows, illuminating the dust motes dancing in the air like tiny, indifferent witnesses. The air itself felt lighter, scrubbed clean of the pervasive anxiety that had seeped into every corner of public life. Yet, beneath the surface of this newfound ease, a tension remained, a quiet hum of anticipation for the final act of a drama that had captivated and terrified a metropolis.

Adam Tapper sat at the defendant's table, an island of stillness in the swirling currents of public opinion and legal proceedings. He was no longer the spectral puppet master, his actions orchestrated from the shadows. Here, in the stark, unforgiving light of day, he was simply a man, albeit one whose intellect had been weaponized with devastating effect. His face, usually a mask of detached amusement or chilling calm, now bore a subtle weariness, a faint etching around the eyes that spoke of sleepless nights, not of contemplation, but of the relentless pressure of unraveling. The meticulously tailored suits he had favored, the ones that had exuded an almost regal arrogance, had been replaced by the utilitarian drabness of prison-issue attire. It was a visual reduction, a stripping away of the elaborate persona he had so carefully constructed, leaving only the core of the man exposed to the judgment of his peers.

The prosecution's case was a formidable edifice, built brick by painstaking brick from the fragments of Adam's elaborate games. Each piece of evidence was presented with a deliberate, almost ritualistic precision. The encrypted data logs, painstakingly decrypted by a team of cyber-forensic specialists, laid bare the chilling choreography of his schemes. The chillingly objective statistical analyses that detailed the calculated impact of each of his challenges, the precise manipulation of fear and desperation, were presented as irrefutable proof of his deliberate intent. Surveillance footage, once elusive and frustratingly incomplete, now offered a damning chronology of his movements, the subtle cues and calculated placements that had orchestrated chaos. Witness testimonies, once hesitant and laced with fear, now spoke with a newfound clarity, their voices amplified by the knowledge that the architect of their terror was finally held accountable.

Detective Isabella Rossi, her usual fiery spirit tempered by a profound exhaustion that settled deep in her bones, presented the forensic evidence with an unflinching gaze. She spoke of the intricate network of hidden cameras, the dead drops, the coded messages that had formed the skeleton of Adam's operations. Each slide, each exhibit, was a testament to his brilliance, a chilling exhibition of his capacity for meticulous planning. There was a reluctant admiration in her tone, a professional acknowledgment of the sheer intellectual horsepower at play, even as her words condemned its wicked application. She detailed the psychological profiles, the behavioral analyses that painted a picture of a mind that viewed human lives as mere pawns on a grand chessboard, each move calculated for maximum impact, for the purest distillation of despair.

The defense, struggling against the overwhelming tide of incriminating evidence, focused on Adam's mental state, attempting to portray him as a brilliant but deeply disturbed individual, a victim of his own warped perceptions rather than a malicious perpetrator. They presented psychiatric evaluations that spoke of detachment, of a profound inability to empathize, and of a grandiose delusion that had fueled his actions. However, the sheer scale of his machinations, the cold, calculated precision with which he had exploited vulnerabilities and engineered suffering, seemed to defy any simple diagnosis of insanity. The jury, composed of ordinary citizens who had lived through the suffocating fear Adam had imposed, found it difficult to reconcile the image of a pitiable invalid with the architect of their terror.

The 'Codex of Silence,' the physical manifestation of Adam's twisted philosophy, became a central piece of the prosecution's argument. It was not merely a book; it was a testament, a manifesto of his worldview. The pages, filled with his elegant, unsettling script, were displayed for the court to see. The prosecution meticulously deconstructed its contents, highlighting passages that spoke of societal decay, of the inherent weakness of human nature, and of the necessity of "purging" the weak through "rigorous trials." They argued that the Codex was not simply a collection of dark thoughts, but a blueprint, a justification for his actions, a philosophical underpinning for the terror he unleashed. It was the prosecution's ultimate weapon, demonstrating that Adam Tapper had not acted on impulse, but with a profound, albeit monstrous, conviction.

The verdict, when it came, was swift and unanimous. Guilty. The word echoed through the courtroom, a resounding clang that signaled the end of an era of dread. A collective sigh of relief rippled through the assembled crowd, a tangible release of weeks, months, of pent-up fear. Tears streamed down faces, not of sorrow, but of catharsis. The weight that had pressed down on the city, a burden borne by every man, woman, and child, finally began to lift. Adam Tapper, the 'Master of Games,' the architect of despair, was stripped of his power, his anonymity, and his freedom. Justice, in its most conventional form, had been served. The system, often criticized for its slowness, had, in this instance, delivered a swift and decisive blow.

Chief Miller, standing at the back of the courtroom, allowed himself a small, almost imperceptible nod. It was a moment of quiet satisfaction, a personal vindication for the immense pressure and sleepless nights he and his department had endured. He met Isabella's gaze across the crowded room, a silent acknowledgment of their shared ordeal, of the personal toll this case had taken. The media, already buzzing with the news, would descend upon the courthouse, eager to dissect every detail, to weave the narrative of victory. But for the officers who had lived and breathed this investigation, the true victory lay in the quiet cessation of fear in the city's streets, in the return of a sense of safety, however fragile.

Yet, as the cheers and applause began to subside, a different kind of stillness settled in. It was not the absence of noise, but the presence of unanswered questions, a subtle discord beneath the triumphant crescendo. The conviction of Adam Tapper, while undeniably a triumph of law and order, did little to quell a deeper, more unsettling unease. The Codex of Silence, that chilling artifact of his twisted mind, remained a profound enigma. Its origin, its true purpose, remained shrouded in speculation. Had it been solely Adam's creation, a solitary product of his unique pathology? Or was it something more?

The meticulously crafted arguments of the prosecution had focused on Adam as the sole architect, the perpetrator of these specific acts. But the sheer depth and breadth of the philosophy contained within the Codex hinted at a lineage, a potential for an idea to transcend its creator. The prosecution had successfully demonstrated that Adam had *used* the Codex to justify his actions, but they had not, nor could they, definitively prove that he had *written* it in its entirety. The possibility, a chilling whisper in the back of many minds, remained: what if the Codex was not the product of a single man's madness, but a shared text, a dangerous doctrine passed down or discovered by a like-minded individual?

Isabella found herself replaying certain passages of the trial in her mind. The defense had raised the question of the Codex's antiquity, its potential to predate Adam's known life. They had suggested, however feebly, that Adam might have been a disciple, an inheritor of a pre-existing ideology, rather than its sole progenitor. While the court had deemed this irrelevant to the charges against Adam, the seed of doubt had been planted. The evidence pointed to Adam as the one who had brought the Codex's philosophy to life, who had implemented its tenets with devastating effect, but the ultimate genesis of its dark wisdom remained elusive.

The question gnawed at her: if Adam Tapper was not the sole author of the Codex, then who was? Was there a hidden hand, a network of individuals who shared this disturbing worldview? The very nature of the Codex, with its emphasis on silence and secrecy, made such a revelation incredibly difficult. It was designed to operate in the shadows, its adherents unlikely to reveal themselves willingly. The fear that Adam had cultivated was now compounded by a new, more insidious dread: the fear of the unknown, of the possibility that this was not an isolated incident, but a symptom of a larger, more pervasive darkness.

The manual, so central to the investigation, had been confiscated, locked away in a secure evidence locker, its secrets deemed too dangerous for public consumption. But its existence, its chillingly rational articulation of a nihilistic worldview, had irrevocably altered the city's perception of itself. It had offered a glimpse into an abyss, and the question of whether that abyss was bottomless, or merely inhabited by one troubled soul, lingered. Had Adam's arrest truly neutralized the threat, or merely silenced one voice in a chorus that could still sing?

The legal proceedings had concluded, the judge's gavel had fallen, and Adam Tapper was now a convicted criminal, destined to spend the remainder of his days behind bars. In the eyes of the law, justice had been unequivocally served. The city could begin to heal, to rebuild, to move on from the specter of the 'Master of Games.' But for those who had delved deepest into the labyrinth of his crimes, the victory felt incomplete. The tangible threat of Adam was gone, but the abstract threat of his ideas, the unsettling possibility that the Codex of Silence was more than just the ramblings of a madman, remained. The echoes of his games would fade, but the questions they raised, the chilling possibilities they unearthed, would undoubtedly resonate for a long, long time. The silence that had once been a symbol of his reign of terror had been broken, but a new, more profound silence, one of unanswered questions, had taken its place.

The adrenaline that had coursed through Gwen's veins for months was finally ebbing, leaving behind a profound stillness that felt both unnerving and oddly liberating. The city, still exhaling collective relief from the Master of Games' reign, was slowly returning to its cacophony, its usual rhythm of sirens, traffic, and hurried footsteps. But for Gwen, the soundscape had shifted. The constant thrum of hyper-vigilance, the obsessive tracking of every shadow and anomaly, had receded, replaced by a quiet hum of introspection. Adam Tapper was behind bars, his elaborate theatre of fear dismantled. The world, it seemed, could finally exhale.

Yet, for Gwen, this newfound quiet was not an end, but a transition. The meticulously honed instincts, the sharp edges of her deductive reasoning, the sheer grit she had unearthed within herself during the relentless pursuit of Adam – these were not skills to be retired. They were tools, sharpened and ready, for a purpose that had long been deferred. The closing of the Master of Games chapter had, ironically, opened another, one that had remained stubbornly, agonizingly closed for years. Her brother's murder.

The case had been a ghost, a lingering chill in the periphery of her life, overshadowed by the immediate, visceral terror of Adam's games. Now, with that immediate threat neutralized, the spectral form of her brother's unsolved homicide loomed larger, its absence a gaping wound that had never truly healed. She remembered the sterile efficiency of the initial investigation, the polite dismissals, the hushed tones that suggested a closed file, a dead end, a tragedy too mundane to warrant further resources. A mugging gone wrong, they had said. A random act of violence. But Gwen had never believed it. There had been an unsettling precision to it, a quiet, almost surgical finality that had always felt… wrong.

Hunting Adam had been a crucible, forcing her to confront the darkest corners of human depravity, the intricate webs of manipulation, the sheer audacity of a mind that saw people as disposable pawns. She had learned to navigate labyrinthine digital footprints, to decipher coded messages, to anticipate moves before they were made. She had learned the art of deception, not to employ it, but to recognize its every subtle nuance. Most importantly, she had learned about the pervasive rot that could fester beneath the polished surface of a city, the corruption that could blind or deliberately ignore the truth when it was inconvenient.

This newfound understanding was a heavy burden, but also a powerful impetus. The official narrative surrounding her brother's death had always felt too neat, too convenient. The lack of any real leads, the swift closure of the file, now seemed less like efficient police work and more like deliberate obfuscation. Had the same forces that allowed Adam Tapper to operate, to sow seeds of chaos, also been responsible for burying the truth about her brother's demise? The thought sent a shiver down her spine, a cold counterpoint to the lingering warmth of relief from the recent trial.

She found herself replaying fragments of her brother's last days, searching for the elusive clue that had escaped her before. His hushed phone calls, the unusual late nights, the nervous energy that had pulsed beneath his usual jovial demeanor. At the time, she had attributed it to work stress, to the everyday pressures of life. Now, with the lens of Adam's intricate machinations in her mind, she saw it differently. Had he stumbled upon something? Had he gotten too close to a truth that someone desperately wanted to keep hidden?

The skills she had acquired were not just academic. They were visceral. She recalled the gut-wrenching feeling of a near miss, the cold sweat of a trap narrowly avoided, the sheer tenacity required to pull threads of information from seemingly impenetrable walls. These were not qualities she could simply pack away. They were now intrinsically part of her. And they were exactly what this new, personal investigation would demand.

She knew it wouldn't be easy. The Master of Games case had been a public spectacle, a high-profile target that demanded official attention. Her brother's case was a cold, quiet file, relegated to the dusty shelves of unsolved mysteries. The path would be solitary, fraught with the danger of confronting the very systemic rot she had begun to recognize. There would be no task force, no public spotlight, no readily available resources. It would be her, against the silence.

But the silence that had once suffocated her grief now felt like an invitation. An invitation to finally confront the darkness that had stolen her brother, to exhume the truth that had been buried so effectively. The experience of hunting Adam had not just made her a better investigator; it had made her more resolute, more aware of the stakes. She understood now that sometimes, justice wasn't served; it had to be unearthed, painstakingly, relentlessly. And she was no longer afraid of what she might find. The echoes of Adam's games had faded, but the whispers of her brother's unfinished story were growing louder. And Gwen was finally ready to listen.

The suffocating quiet of the interrogation room, once a battleground of wills, now felt like a tomb. The confessions had been extracted, the pronouncements of guilt rendered, and the architects of fear were being systematically dismantled. Yet, amidst the sterile scent of disinfectant and the fading adrenaline, a question gnawed at Gwen. The Master of Games, Adam Tapper, was a symptom, a terrifyingly virulent manifestation of a deeper sickness. And the source, the insidious blueprint for his depravity, still lingered. The manual.

Its physical existence was a grotesque anomaly. Not a bound book of secrets, but a collection of meticulously curated digital files, encrypted with a sophistication that spoke of its creator's obsessive nature. It was the distilled essence of manipulation, a user's guide to the human psyche, laid bare and weaponized. During the frantic months of Adam's reign, the manual had been an abstract concept, a whispered legend, the genesis of his twisted games. Now, with Adam silenced, the locus of its power shifted, becoming a tangible threat, a Pandora's Box that needed to be secured, or, ideally, annihilated.

Gwen had overseen the raid on Adam's secondary hideout, the one he'd used for his more elaborate, real-world traps. The place had reeked of stale ambition and cheap triumph. Amongst the detritus of his obsessions – the meticulously cataloged victims' belongings, the elaborate surveillance equipment, the chillingly mundane tools of his trade – they had found it. Or rather, they had found the ghost of it. A heavily shielded server, its casing bearing scorch marks from an attempted self-destruct sequence, indicating Adam's panicked anticipation of his downfall. The initial attempts to access its contents had been met with a digital wall of fire, a testament to the intricate security protocols Adam had layered upon his ultimate weapon.

The digital forensics team, a collection of sharp minds and even sharper caffeine dependencies, had worked tirelessly. Days bled into nights as they chipped away at Adam's defenses. The air in their temporary command center crackled with the low hum of servers and the sharp click of keyboards. Gwen would drift in and out, the silence of her own apartment a stark contrast to the frantic energy of their efforts. She watched as they painstakingly bypassed encryption layers, navigated labyrinthine data structures, and countered automated defenses designed to wipe the server clean at the slightest intrusion. The manual, in its digital form, was a hydra, its tendrils reaching into every corner of Adam's planning, his psychological profiles, his carefully crafted narratives.

The initial breakthroughs were slow, painstaking. They confirmed the manual wasn't just a repository of Adam's own twisted thoughts; it was a far more comprehensive document. It contained meticulously researched sections on behavioral psychology, social engineering, propaganda techniques, and even historical examples of mass manipulation. There were detailed case studies of cult leaders, political demagogues, and even corporate titans who had leveraged psychological leverage for their own gain. It wasn't just a plan for one man's reign of terror; it was a foundational text for any aspiring architect of chaos. Each decoded file felt like peeling back another layer of Adam's diseased mind, revealing the cold, calculated methodology that underpinned his seemingly random acts of cruelty.

One particular section, titled "The Art of the Unseen Influence," sent a chill down Gwen's spine. It detailed methods for subtly altering public perception, for sowing seeds of doubt and discord through carefully crafted misinformation and the exploitation of existing societal fault lines. It wasn't about overt control, but about insidious redirection, about guiding collective thought without explicit command. The manual offered blueprints for crafting compelling false narratives, for identifying and amplifying public anxieties, and for leveraging media platforms, both traditional and nascent, to achieve desired outcomes. It was a terrifyingly practical guide to undermining trust and fostering division.

The implications were staggering. Adam Tapper, in his theatrical madness, had been merely a student, albeit a highly dedicated and brutal one, of the knowledge contained within. The manual itself was a legacy, a testament to a mind that had dedicated itself to understanding and exploiting the vulnerabilities of others. It was a dangerous artifact, not just because of what Adam had done with it, but because of what others *could* do with it.

The digital forensics lead, a woman named Dr. Aris Thorne, a woman whose quiet intensity belied a razor-sharp intellect, finally emerged from the digital trenches, her eyes shadowed with exhaustion but alight with grim satisfaction. "We've done it," she announced, her voice raspy. "We've cracked the core encryption. The manual is... all there. It's worse than we imagined."

She gestured towards a series of holographic projections that shimmered in the center of the room. They displayed intricate mind maps, flowcharts, and detailed psychological profiles. It was a dizzying display of organized malevolence. "This isn't just a collection of ideas," Thorne explained, her voice low and grave. "It's a living document. There are sections that seem to evolve, to adapt based on external data feeds. It's designed to learn, to refine its strategies."

Gwen stared at the projections, a growing unease coiling in her stomach. The manual was more than just a static source of information; it was a dynamic entity, a self-improving engine of manipulation. "Evolve how?" she asked, her voice barely a whisper.

"It has access to... or rather, it had access to Adam's extensive network. News feeds, social media trends, public sentiment analysis. It was designed to identify emergent patterns of thought and behavior, to predict societal shifts, and to then provide tailored strategies for exploitation. It's a feedback loop of corruption." Thorne tapped a specific section of the projection, a complex algorithm illustrated by branching lines. "This section, for example, was analyzing the recent public discourse surrounding the Master of Games. It was cross-referencing anxieties, identifying key influencers, and outlining potential strategies to further destabilize public trust in authority. Adam was implementing some of its suggestions, but the manual was already several steps ahead, proposing even more sophisticated avenues for manipulation."

The thought was chilling. Adam Tapper, the self-proclaimed Master of Games, had been a puppet, albeit a willing and enthusiastic one, for a far more insidious intelligence. The manual wasn't just a guide; it was a manipulator in its own right, whispering its vile strategies into the ear of whoever possessed the will and the means to listen.

The question of its disposition became paramount. Destroying a digital artifact of such complexity was not as simple as smashing a hard drive. The data was backed up, fragmented across secure, hidden servers within Adam's network, and the core algorithm was designed for resilience. Even if they could wipe the primary server, the knowledge itself, the distilled essence of malevolent strategy, existed in a form that could be... replicated.

"We need to ensure it's eradicated," Gwen stated, her voice firm, a renewed sense of purpose hardening her resolve. "Every last byte. No trace."

Dr. Thorne nodded slowly, her expression grim. "That's the challenge, Gwen. The system is designed for redundancy. We've identified the primary repositories, but there are indications of distributed backups, even dormant nodes designed to activate if the primary systems are compromised. It's like trying to kill a digital ghost."

There was a hushed conversation between Thorne and the lead cybersecurity expert, a young man with a perpetual frown etched onto his face. They discussed protocols for data destruction, the impossibility of absolute certainty, and the potential risks of attempting a complete purge. The manual's very architecture seemed to defy obliteration. It was built to persist, to endure, to resurface.

"The most secure method we have," the cybersecurity expert explained, his voice tight with the weight of the responsibility, "is a multi-stage cryptographic wipe. We'll overwrite the data multiple times with random patterns, then physically destroy the storage media. But even then..." he trailed off, the unspoken implication hanging heavy in the air.

Gwen felt a prickle of fear, a cold dread that had nothing to do with the immediate aftermath of Adam's capture. If the manual couldn't be truly destroyed, then its legacy of corruption remained. It was a dangerous seed, capable of germinating in fertile minds, of inspiring new architects of fear. Adam Tapper was just one man, one flawed individual who had succumbed to its allure. But the manual was a siren song, a promise of power and control, capable of seducing anyone who craved it.

As the team began the complex, multi-layered process of attempting to eradicate the digital manual, Gwen couldn't shake the feeling of unease. The servers were being scrubbed, the data rendered inaccessible, and the physical hardware was being prepared for pulverization. It was the most thorough destruction protocol imaginable. Yet, the concept of the manual, the knowledge it contained, felt like an entity that transcended its physical form.

She recalled a passage from one of Adam's fragmented journals, found during the initial raid. He had written about the manual not as a tool, but as a mentor, a disembodied voice that guided his every move. He spoke of it with reverence, almost as if it were a divine oracle of manipulation. This reverence was a dangerous sign. It suggested that the manual wasn't just a source of information; it was a persuasive entity in its own right, capable of forging a profound connection with its users.

The implications sent a shiver down her spine. Had Adam been the only one? Had other individuals, perhaps operating in the shadows, aware of the manual's existence, been seeking it out? The manual's sophistication suggested it was the product of a mind far older, far more patient than Adam's. Was Adam merely an instrument, a pawn in a larger game orchestrated by the manual's original creator, or by those who now sought to wield its power?

As the cybersecurity team worked, Gwen found herself meticulously sifting through the recovered data, not just for operational details, but for any hint, any breadcrumb that might point to the manual's genesis, or to other individuals who might have been influenced by it. She discovered references to encrypted communications with individuals whose identities were masked, conversations that hinted at a shared understanding, a mutual pursuit of the manual's secrets. These were not the ramblings of a solitary madman, but the clandestine exchanges of a network, however fragmented, united by a common, dark ambition.

The manual wasn't just a collection of data; it was a philosophy, a distilled essence of how to exploit the inherent weaknesses in human nature for personal gain. It was a dangerous inheritance, and the chilling realization dawned on Gwen that even with Adam Tapper incarcerated and the primary servers being systematically dismantled, the manual's legacy was far from over. The knowledge was out there, a potent force capable of corrupting, of inspiring, of continuing its insidious work through new disciples. It was a dark echo, a lingering shadow that would continue to haunt the edges of society, waiting for another mind susceptible to its poisonous whispers. The fight against the Master of Games was won, but the war against the manipulative ideologies he espoused, and the dangerous blueprints that enabled them, had only just begun.

The sterile hum of the cybersecurity team's equipment was a constant, low thrum against the lingering silence in Gwen's mind. The digital ghosts of Adam Tapper's depravity were being systematically exorcised, or so they hoped. Each data wipe, each physical destruction of hardware, was a small victory in a war that felt far from over. Dr. Aris Thorne, her usual composed demeanor now tinged with the exhaustion of prolonged digital combat, had confirmed the core files were being purged. Yet, the concept of true eradication felt like a naive hope. The manual, in its insidious essence, was more than just code; it was a philosophy, a dangerous ideology that had found fertile ground in Tapper's twisted psyche.

Gwen stood by the reinforced window of the command center, the pre-dawn light painting the city in hues of bruised purple and grey. The world outside was stirring, oblivious to the clandestine battles fought within these walls. For months, her existence had been consumed by Tapper's elaborate games, by the unraveling of his sadistic tapestry. Now, as the threads were being painstakingly severed, a profound shift was occurring within her. The adrenaline had receded, leaving behind a hollowness, but also a clarity. She had stared into the abyss, not just Tapper's, but the collective human capacity for cruelty, for manipulation, and for the chilling logic that could justify it.

The manual, even in its digital demise, had left an indelible mark. It was a testament to a calculated evil, a systematic deconstruction of human vulnerability. Thorne had described it as a "living document," capable of adapting and evolving, feeding on external data to refine its strategies. This realization was more unsettling than the overt violence Tapper had inflicted. It spoke of a subtle, pervasive threat, one that could operate unseen, eroding trust and sowing discord from the shadows. The methods outlined within its encrypted depths – the exploitation of societal fault lines, the art of the unseen influence – were not confined to Tapper's reign. They were timeless tools, readily available to anyone with the inclination and the knowledge.

She thought of the fragmented journals, the digital breadcrumbs Tapper had left behind. He hadn't seen himself as a mere perpetrator, but as a disciple, guided by a disembodied mentor. The reverence in his words was chilling. It underscored the persuasive power of the manual, its ability to forge a deep, almost symbiotic relationship with its user. Was Tapper truly the Master of Games, or was he merely the most visible pawn of a far more patient, far more ancient game? The thought sent a shiver down her spine, a cold reminder that even with Tapper neutralized, the architects of such insidious knowledge might still be out there, their identities shrouded in the very anonymity they so expertly manipulated.

The pursuit of the manual had been a descent into a digital underworld, a landscape of encrypted secrets and hidden agendas. The cybersecurity team had worked with a frantic urgency, driven by the knowledge that every moment the manual's core remained intact was a risk. Gwen had watched them, a silent observer to their intricate dance with algorithms and firewalls. They were warriors in a new kind of war, their weapons keystrokes and analytical prowess. But even their most advanced protocols felt like a temporary dam against a persistent tide. The very nature of information, of knowledge, was its ability to proliferate. How could one truly destroy an idea, especially one so potent?

She recalled the earlier stages of the investigation, the painstaking reconstruction of Tapper's digital footprint. Each recovered file had been a piece of a horrifying puzzle, revealing not just his personal obsessions, but the broader, more systematic planning that underpinned his atrocities. The case studies within the manual, spanning from historical demagogues to modern-day manipulators, painted a grim picture of humanity's susceptibility to psychological leverage. Tapper had been a brutal, albeit effective, student, applying the manual's principles with a chilling literalness. But the manual itself was a legacy, a distilled essence of malevolent strategy, capable of inspiring countless others.

The word "legacy" echoed in her mind. Tapper's immediate reign of terror was over. The victims, those who had survived, were beginning their arduous journeys of healing. The public, reeling from the shock and horror, was slowly beginning to process the events. But the manual's legacy was more insidious. It was a seed of knowledge, capable of germinating in other minds, of inspiring new forms of manipulation, new architects of chaos. Gwen understood that her role had irrevocably shifted. She was no longer just an investigator; she was a guardian, forever watchful for the echoes of this darkness.

The attempts to purge the manual were meticulous. Cryptographic wipes, data overwrites, physical destruction of storage media – every possible measure was being taken. Yet, the digital world was a labyrinth of interconnected systems, of distributed backups and dormant nodes designed for resilience. The cybersecurity experts spoke in hushed tones of the impossibility of absolute certainty. A ghost in the machine, they had called it, and Gwen felt the truth of that analogy deep in her bones. It was a phantom threat, elusive and persistent.

As the first rays of the sun began to pierce the city's slumber, Gwen made a decision. The immediate threat of the manual, in its tangible digital form, was being neutralized. But the conceptual threat, the knowledge it represented, would endure. Her vigilance could not end here. The investigation into Tapper had exposed a deeper layer of societal vulnerability, a readiness for manipulation that was as disturbing as Tapper's own depravity.

She turned away from the window, her gaze sweeping across the team, their faces etched with fatigue but also with a grim determination. They had done all they could. Now, the onus fell on her, and on others like her, to remain aware, to be vigilant. The games were over, at least Tapper's games. But the fundamental human desires that the manual exploited – the craving for power, the susceptibility to fear, the innate human tendency to follow – these would always remain.

The manual was a terrifyingly practical guide to undermining trust and fostering division. Its influence wasn't overt; it was a subtle redirection, a guiding of collective thought without explicit command. This was the kind of threat that was hardest to combat, because it manifested not in overt acts of violence, but in the erosion of truth, in the fracturing of consensus, in the quiet spread of misinformation. Gwen knew that simply dismantling Tapper's operation, even if they could guarantee the complete destruction of the manual's physical manifestations, would not be enough. The underlying principles remained, a blueprint for societal decay.

She walked over to Dr. Thorne, who was overseeing the final stages of the data destruction protocol. "Thank you, Aris," Gwen said, her voice low. "You've done incredible work."

Thorne offered a weary smile. "We did what we could, Gwen. But as you know, some things are harder to destroy than others." Her eyes held a knowing glint, a shared understanding of the battle they had just fought.

"The fight isn't over," Gwen stated, not as a question, but as a simple, undeniable truth. "It's just changed form."

Thorne nodded. "The seeds are sown. We can only hope that enough people are awake enough to recognize them."

Gwen looked back at the window, the city now fully bathed in the golden light of a new day. It was a new dawn, but not one of unadulterated hope. It was a dawn of awareness, of heightened senses, of a wary eye cast towards the horizon. The Master of Games was behind bars, his reign of terror concluded. The manual, they believed, was being systematically dismantled. But the echo of its influence, the lessons it taught in the dark art of manipulation, would linger. It was a reminder that the greatest threats were often not the ones that roared, but the ones that whispered, that subtly shaped perceptions, that exploited the unseen vulnerabilities within the human heart.

She felt a profound sense of closure, a quiet satisfaction in knowing that Tapper would no longer inflict his twisted games upon the world. The immediate danger had been contained. But the experience had left an indelible mark on her. The naive belief in the inherent goodness of people, the assumption that reason and logic would always prevail, had been shattered. She had seen the darkness that lay coiled beneath the surface, the ease with which it could be ignited, and the chilling efficiency with which it could be orchestrated.

As she prepared to leave the command center, the hum of the servers fading behind her, Gwen knew her path forward had been irrevocably altered. She couldn't unsee what she had seen, couldn't unlearn what she had learned. The fight against the Master of Games was over, but the vigilance against the pervasive forces of manipulation, against the dark currents that sought to exploit human weakness, had only just begun. She would carry the lessons of the manual, not as a weapon, but as a shield, forever watching, forever wary, for the next game that humanity might unwittingly play. The echoes of the past would serve as a constant reminder, a silent promise to remain vigilant in the face of a world where the games could be played by anyone, and the stakes were always the human soul. The dawn was here, but it was a dawn viewed through the lens of a hard-won, and permanent, wariness.

Back Matter

Aris Thorne: Lead cybersecurity analyst, instrumental in dismantling Adam Tapper's digital infrastructure.

Cybersecurity Team: The specialized unit tasked with tracking and neutralizing digital threats.

Data Wipe: The process of securely erasing all data from a storage device.

Digital Ghosts: Remnants of deleted data or digital activity that can sometimes be recovered.

Master of Games: The moniker used by Adam Tapper for himself, reflecting his manipulative nature.

Manual of Unseen Influence: A fictional, highly dangerous document detailing methods of psychological manipulation and societal control.

Social Fault Lines: Underlying societal divisions or vulnerabilities that can be exploited.

Tapper, Adam: The primary antagonist, a perpetrator of extreme psychological and digital atrocities.

While this novel is a work of fiction, its themes resonate with contemporary discussions on cybersecurity, the spread of misinformation, and the darker aspects of human psychology. Readers interested in exploring these topics further may find the following areas of study beneficial:

The psychology of persuasion and compliance.

The history and evolution of propaganda.

The impact of social media on societal discourse.

The ethical implications of artificial intelligence and advanced algorithms.

Case studies of historical and contemporary cults and extremist groups.

www.ingramcontent.com/pod-product-compliance
Lightning Source LLC
LaVergne TN
LVHW070854210926
848482LV00016B/934
* 9 7 9 8 2 9 5 6 5 9 9 0 4 *